BIRDS OF THE WORLD

EL SIETE COLOR

Regulus omnicolor Vieill.

Gay pinx. Imp. de Lorauvage. Guyard sculp.

H. Aramata

BIRDS OF THE WORLD

AS PAINTED BY 19TH-CENTURY ARTISTS

Outarde   Bécasseau   Cigogne   Poule d'eau   Pétrel   Pélican   Canard   Manchot

Crown Publishers, Inc.
New York

Opposite the frontispiece, kinglet calyptura (Calyptura cristata, *Passeriformes, Cotingidae*), *from Gay, 1844-71 (19).*

The illustrations in this book are from the Aramata Collection
Scientific consultation for the international edition by
Professor Renato Massa
Texts: Renato Massa and Carlo Violani
Editorial director: Lorenzo Camusso

First published in the United States by Crown Publishers, Inc., 201 East 50 Street, New York, New York 10022 and simultaneously in Canada by General Publishing Company.

CROWN is a trademark of Crown Publishers, Inc.

Manufactured in Italy

ISBN 0-517-573741

Library of Congress Catalog Card Number 89-62240

10 9 8 7 6 5 4 3 2 1

First American edition

Contents

NATURALISTS AND ARTISTS:

Ornithology Adventurously Draws the Catalog of the Species

Perroquet   Aigle   G^d Duc   Guacharo

"ORIGINS" AND "MIRACLES": THE STORY OF THIS BOOK

While the animal illustrations in this book were originally produced in Europe and America during the eighteenth and nineteenth centuries, this volume was originally published in the island country of Japan, in the distant reaches of East Asia.

All steps of the original book's production, from the collection of illustrations, to writing of accompanying texts, determination of scientific names, and even the final editing, were performed by a single individual, myself. While acting as both author and editor, I am neither independently wealthy nor a professional naturalist with free access to national museums and university libraries. Until very recently, I was a computer programmer and systems engineer who worked in the data processing department of a marine industries company, a single man with an interest in natural history who moonlighted by translating English works dealing with fantasy and the "occult."

Why did such a poorly equipped person, on a small island in the Far East, come to the decision to edit a work which would so obviously necessitate an enormous expenditure of time and money? Why did I wish to assemble this collection of old, rare animal illustrations now found only in museums like those of Paris and London? Since there will no doubt be a number of readers in the West who find such questions a bit puzzling, let me begin by speaking about the origins of this book.

In Japanese, one possible rendering of the term origin *is the word* engi, *formed from two Sino-Japanese characters. The first character,* en, *means to establish a destined connection or relationship. For example, when a man and a woman meet for the first time, fall in love, and decide to marry, the resulting marriage is said to be an* engumi *or "destined match"; an* en *(relationship) has been consummated.*

On the other hand, the second character, ki *or* gi, *means to arise or begin. When the two characters are combined, the resulting word,* engi, *means to "initiate an* en" *or begin a destined relationship — in other words, to form a deep, sympathetic connection with someone or something. And by extension, the term can be used to signify the "origins" of an event or thing. As a result, this book can be said to have had its own beginnings in the establishing of several mysterious "connections" in the sense of the* engi *spoken of here.*

The first engi *relating to this book is the link of understanding and friendship established between Japan and Europe through the discipline of natural history. Beginning with Linnaeus (1707-1778), the early modern study of natural history focused on making nature surveys and topographical studies which extended around the globe. Linnaeus's prize pupil Carl Peter Thunberg had already visited Japan by 1755, providing a tremendous stimulus to naturalists within Japan. By the first half of the nineteenth century, when Philipp Franz von Siebold (1796-1866) arrived in Japan, a network established between Japanese and European naturalists resulted in the importation of numerous important works dealing with natural history, including those by such authors as Athanasius Kircher (1602-1680), Johannes (John) Jonstons (1603-1675), Johann Wilhelm Weinmann, Etienne Lacépède (1756-1825), and Cornelis Nozemann (1721-1785). These connections are merely one sign of the simultaneous flowering in interest among naturalists around the world. Siebold's own fascination with Japan went so far as to lead him to take a Japanese wife named Otaki, whose name he gave to a Japanese flower, the* Hydrangea otaksa.

One of the most prolific Japanese naturalists of this period was Hiraga Gennai (1729-1779). Hiraga sold his family fortune in order to purchase the naturalist illustrations of Jonstons, and based on those copper-engraved animal prints, he pioneered the study of Western painting in Japan.

*One can say that by the end of Japan's Edo period (ca. 1600-1867), Japan was already firmly linked to the West via a common "connection" (*en*), namely that established through the medium of natural history. Following the Meiji Restoration (1868), however, Japan underwent its own academic revolution. In the process, the discipline of natural history was abandoned as obsolete, and the accompanying "network" between Japan and Europe likewise gradually grew cold.*

I have discovered a great interest in the study of natural history in both the West and Japan during the eighteenth and nineteenth centuries. My fascination with this period in the study of natural history is a result of the effervescent, youthful curiosity and wonder toward all things natural that is evidenced in every aspect of the discipline at that time: the unaffected awe at the beauty of butterflies coupled with the genuine dread of bizarre reptiles and poisonous snakes. In turn, this kind of initial reaction changes at a subsequent stage to a natural kind of intellectual curiosity. And the clearest expression of this process is to be seen in the beautiful, hand-colored plates of animals produced during this era.

A second "connection" linked to the origin of this book is the fortuitous way in which I first came upon these old animal illustrations. Some ten or more years ago, I was browsing through the used book stores which can be found near the campus of Tokyo University, itself site of the oldest zoological and botanical department among Japanese universities. On the shelf of a certain store specializing in old medical texts, I found an old, worn book covered in dust. It was one in the famous twenty-volume series Le Règne Animal, by the distinguished French naturalist Georges Cuvier (1769-1832). The volume in question was a collection of text and illustrations dealing with zoophytes and fish. Although I opened the volume casually and with no special interest, I was suddenly seized with delight as my eye found the skillfully executed and hand-colored copper lithographic prints.

About the same time, I was looking one day through the used book stores in Tokyo's well-known Kanda district — an area where rare books are as common as cabbages at a market — when I came across a collection of colored wood-block prints of fish by Ōno Bakufū, a print artist who carries on the tradition of Edo-period Japanese wood-block printing. Viewing this collection of prints gave me a second shock. I was convinced I had stumbled upon what could only be called a lost art form.

Unfortunately, I could find virtually no one in Japan at that time with an interest in natural history. Even in the arts I could find no one interested in the history of these old naturalist illustrations. Against this background, I could only believe that my chance encounter with these original naturalist prints from both Japan and the West signified a significant en or momentous "connection" which I was meant to have with this lost art form because the Japanese concept of en also involves the sense of one's fate or destiny.

As a result, I decided to embark on a program of writing in an attempt to revive the zoological and botanical lore preserved within the antiquated discipline of natural history, and if possible to stimulate a reevaluation of these old naturalist illustrations. It seems that one characteristic of Japanese like myself is that when they become convinced of a personal en or "destiny," they are converted straightaway into confirmed zealots.

Somewhat paradoxically, I had the advantage here of an interest in both Western and Oriental magic and occult sciences dating from my university days. These fields naturally included many aspects allied to the old discipline of natural history, for example, avian divination, pharmacology, alchemy, and the symbolism of dragons and other phantasmic animals.

At the same time, a number of significant obstacles stood in the way of my pet project. First was the problem of how to gain access to the original editions of the naturalist illustrations I needed. Not only are these works extremely hard to find, but they also demanded prices which were totally beyond my means. As one example, even assuming it was available for sale, an original set of J.J. Audubon's The Birds of America would have cost upwards of 100 million yen, the equivalent of about $740,000 (U.S.) at current rates of exchange. It is said a set of these books was presented to the Tokugawa Shogun by Commodore Perry at the time he sailed into Tokyo Bay in the 1850s, but the present whereabouts of the works are unknown. No original editions of Audubon's illustrations existed in Japan, and it is for this reason that it was not possible to include Audubon's illustrations within the present volume. The difficulty was not limited to Audubon, however. It was an extremely difficult task to even find the other original works which I needed as well. As a result, I spent several years traveling to Europe and America, searching through book stores and establishing connections with large used-book dealers. For example, I was aided in my search by the dealers Bernard Quaritch and Henry Sotheran of London, Weldon & Whesley in the London suburbs, in Paris by Martinez and Rousseau Girard, and in Amsterdam by Antiquariaat Junk. I feel an unrepayable debt of gratitude to these firms even now.

The second obstacle I experienced was in finding the funds which would allow me to purchase the high-priced original works necessary for my project. I have enjoyed collecting books since my childhood, and have even been known to forgo meals in order to apply the extra money to my obessional hobby. But even so, a part-time translator and computer programmer like myself has financial limits. As my monthy expenses for books flowed out like water, I finally came to the unsavory end of going to loan sharks to finance my book purchases. At that rate, I would have ended up myself as a permanent fixture in the abyss before my pet project of resurrecting history would ever have had a chance of seeing the light of day.

In the end I found myself gazing one day at the price listed in Bernard Quaritch's catalog for Levaillant's Historie Naturelle de Oiseaux du Paradis *(The Natural History of the Birds of Paradise)*. It was an enormous sum, far beyond the means of any ordinary individual. I found myself in tears at the realization that I would never be able to buy such a costly book.

But some five years later, a "miracle" occurred in my life. As a minor diversion I wrote an occult novel called Teito monogatari *(Tale of the imperial capital)*, and to my surprise it became a best seller. Set in the Tokyo of Japan's Meiji period *(1868-1912)*, this fantasy romance was a blend of science, magic, and battles to the death, with a protagonist closely resembling the English occultist Aleister Crowley *(1875-1947)*. Against my most optimistic expectations, this book sold some three million copies, and was even the basis for a feature motion picture utilizing special effects photography *(released in January 1988)*. Needless to say, the result of all this unexpected popularity was that I overnight came into an enormous windfall income. And with the money produced by that magic, I was finally able to buy not only the work by Levaillant but virtually all of the other books of naturalist illustrations which I had desired for so long.

And this, in short, is the story of the "origins" and "miracles" lying behind the book you now hold.

— HIROSHI ARAMATA

NATURAL HISTORY IN AN AGE WHEN MEN DISCOURSED WITH BIRDS

In the Japanese version of this book, the legends and folklore associated with names of birds were detailed for over two hundred entries, based largely on the unit of the bird's genus. But when editing the work for European languages it was decided that, since most of the information was related to China and Japan, the translation of the text would prove a colossal task, with the result that Western editions of the work have omitted all the textual material included in the Japanese version.

At the same time, it may be helpful to the Western reader to possess an understanding of the perspective from which the compiler edited this work. As a result, I want here to present my own personal views regarding the discipline of natural history and its significance.

The understanding and knowledge of birds collected in this book was a product of the now antiquated discipline of natural history. In that understanding was implied the wisdom of an age when humans and birds were viewed within a relationship of equality. As an inevitable result, the nature of that knowledge is at variance with the understanding found in the modern discipline of ornithology. This because natural history was neither a strict science in the modern sense of the term, nor merely a simple collection of folklore. It was an understanding born from a consideration of birds as having rational, social qualities on a par with those same features found among human beings. And in all likelihood that fact forms the essence of ornithology as expressed within the old discipline of natural history. Natural historians were participants in a body of knowledge closely allied to that systematic study of useful, efficacious plants and herbs which was called "physical botany." As regards birds they were, in short, engaged in the study of what might be termed "humanistic ornithology."

As a result, the "birds" that are treated here are not merely birds within a "natural" topography, but birds considered from within a human cultural topography as well. Beginning with sparrows and ostriches, the realm of "birds" extended as well to the mythical garuda and phoenix. Even real birds like the sparrow, however, were treated not only from within the perspective of their natural habitat, but from a human cultural frame as well. In other words, it might be said that the object of study extended not only to living and dead mounted sparrows, but even to nonexisting sparrows and thence to those sparrows related through oral accounts and the depictions of art.

The knowledge of natural history contained in this volume arises from two sources. One is, of course, the fruit of those natural historians who dedicated their entire lives to the study of birds. But the other is the lore transmitted by people who were thought able to communicate directly with birds, through access to magical powers. This volume has placed special emphasis on this latter form of knowledge, the result of a conviction that information about birds is best received directly from the mouths of the birds themselves.

Along these lines, let me make reference first to the story of "Solomon's Ring" well known from the title of an essay by the zoologist Konrad Lorenz. According to Jewish legend, David's son King Solomon (ca. 1000 B.C.E.) was known not only for his great wisdom and wealth, but also for his ability to converse with animals. And it is said that that power came from a magic ring which he wore. One day, Solomon called all the birds to his palace, and all came with the exception of a young rooster. When the king asked the reason, it was reported that the rooster had gone to visit the idolatrous country ruled by the Queen of Sheba. The rooster later sent word to Solomon that he should send an army of birds to destroy her country.

Numerous variations can be found of legends like this, legends in which heroes are depicted as having the ability to discourse with birds. For example, in the Icelandic Volsunga Saga, the dragon-slayer Sigurd gained the power of understanding the language of birds by tasting the blood of a dragon. St. Francis of Assisi was likewise said to call birds together to preach to them. The question arising from all this legendary material is the meaning of this kind of "discourse with birds."

Birds are often said to "chirp," or what in Japanese is called saezuru. According to the Wakun no shiori ([A Compendium of Japanese Words], 93 volumes, published over a one-hundred-year period beginning in 1777), the term saezuru comes from the term sawarideru, meaning "to be emitted with difficulty." This work goes on to state, "this term is used because birds' speech is impeded and difficult to comprehend." For this same reason, the Japanese of the period called the Korean language karasaezuri, which meant "Chinese chirping." As is clear from these references, birds' speech was considered typical of language which was difficult to comprehend, and it was thus thought that the ability to understand this most difficult speech was equivalent to an ability to understand all the world's languages.

In fact, people of ages past considered the activity of discoursing with the birds a beautiful symbol of an expanding global culture. This because an exchange of information which included the speech of birds — and accordingly the most difficult of languages throughout the world — intimated a knowledge which would become the basis for a new global human culture. And for that very reason a knowledge of birds' names, customs, and language was considered equal to a knowledge of the world.

A number of reasons can be postulated for this belief in the wisdom of birds. Most important is likely the fact that birds were viewed as spiritual beings who traversed the heavens, the space between this world and the other world, the world of human existence and the world of spirit. As a result, they were viewed as rulers of this world, or representatives of divinity.

Birds were considered gods, for example, in ancient Egypt. The god of the moon, Thot, was portrayed as an ibis, while Horus — the god of light — was a falcon, and both gods were viewed as bearers of wisdom regarding the heavenly bodies. When the Greek alphabet was created, it was said that a hint was received from a formation of flying cranes, while an ancient Persian legend stated that men had once been ruled by chickens.

In ancient China, it was said that the mythical Emperor of the West, Shao Hao, had appointed birds as imperial officials when establishing his reign because it was believed birds performed the most ably as ministers and officials. The swallow, shrike, quail, and chicken were given charge over the four seasons, while the phoenix was appointed to the post of prime minister. The chief ministers having charge over the central government were the five birds the dove, eagle, cuckoo, hawk, and one other (whose identity is now unknown) called the hua-chiu (Japanese kakkyū).

The male dove was said to send its mate out of the nest when it rained, and call her back when the rain stopped. With this kind of control of its wife, the dove was thought to be most filial to its parents, and so it was made minister of education. The eagle was brave, with the result that it was made minister of war. The hawk was viewed as strict and selfless, with the result that it was made minister of law. And the hua-chiu (kakkyū) was said to chirp both night and day, and so it was made the court's minister of information. The cuckoo was said to weave its nest in the mulberry tree and skillfully raise seven fledglings, with the result that it was made minister of construction. The irony in this last selection cannot go unnoticed, namely, the fact that "minister of construction" was selected on its ability to raise numerous young within a crowded nest.

In Japanese myth as well, it was said that the first creator gods Izanagi and Izanami were unable to successfully consummate their initial union, with the result that they received instruction from the wagtail. Likewise, when the goddess Toyotama hime was about to give birth she had a parturition house thatched with feathers from the cormorant, which was considered a god of safe childbirth. In turn, her child was called Ugayafukiaezu no Mikoto (interpreted by Aston to mean "Prince-beach-brave-cormorant-rush-thatch-unfinished").

The first avian researchers produced from within this kind of legendary milieu were the "bird diviners." Since birds were viewed as messengers who traveled between this world and the next, it was only natural that they were considered capable of intimate communication with both realms. As a result, people who studied the movements of birds in an effort to divine the messages of the gods were considered penetrating seers led by the wisdom of the birds. In Japan, an example of this kind can be seen in the clan known as Haijshi, makers of tombs and clay objects. The Haijshi were said to be masters of the "long-singing birds of the Eternal Land" (roosters), the same birds which in myth were said to have crowed when the sun goddess Amaterasu hid away in a cave.

But more important in this respect are the bird diviners of ancient Rome. These were three high-ranking officials responsible for divining the national fortune by studying the flight, eating habits, and flocking patterns of birds. It was even said that a bird diviner was called upon to augur which of the two legendary brothers, Romulus or Remus, would be destined to be Rome's first ruler. Twelve sacred birds circled around Romulus, thus revealing the gods' will that he be selected. When performing their bird divinations, the diviners would face south; if birds appeared from the left side, it was considered a good omen. Observations regarding the kind and number of birds appearing were used to make more detailed judgments. The Historia Naturalis (Natural History) of Pliny the Elder (23-79 C.E.) includes observations about birds taken from diviners.

In a few cases, the means used by such diviners were part of an established culture, but most aspects were part of the "occupational secrets" preserved by the diviners themselves. As a result, it is virtually impossible today to reconstruct the precise contours of the procedures involved. We can, however, give an example that illustrates the overall situation. The Greek word ornis ("bird") was also used as a general referent for things having no relation to birds but signifying "auspicious," "prediction," or "good luck." It is said that the term for bad luck, omen, is also derived from a root related to ornis, and these usages were of course the result of the practice of avian divination. As symbols of the wisdom of the other world, birds were thus viewed as sacred and given careful protection. And that role was carried out by kings and lords.

In India of the third century B.C.E., King Asoka prohibited the hunting of parrots and cranes, together with many other animals and birds. In Egypt during the age of the Middle Kingdom, orders were given to restrict the hunting of water birds, while in England, charter laws were established in the twelfth and thirteenth centuries to protect natural forests, including their wild birds and salmon. Henry VIII prohibited the killing of crows (the "Crow Law"), while Elizabeth I prohibited the use of nets for taking pheasants and quail.

In Japan as well, the fifth Tokugawa Shogun Tsunayoshi (1646-1749) issued the "ordinance prohibiting the taking of animal life," with the result that whenever a bird's nest was found in the city of Edo it would be taken down and the young raised by officials charged with this task. The great explosion of bird populations which resulted from this policy forced city officials to take excess birds several times each year for release in various localities outside the city. It is said the shogun took pity on animal life in this way as a means of consoling himself for the fact that he was not blessed with an heir.

The significance of this kind of historical protection and cultivation of birds — an attitude based on a valuing of the divinity of birds — is far easier to understand than many of the slogans of modern animal-protection movements. Thus, the activity of protecting and cultivating animal life and allowing animals to live happily within the context of human society was first and foremost a problem in political science. The reason is that a disappearance of birds from within a king's domain was taken as a sign that there was fault with the king's rule. In other words, the problem of the protection and cultivation of birds was one link in the maintenance of good general relations between "ruler and ruled." From the point of view of the ruler, people, birds, and animals were all beings within essentially the same realm of existence.

Once the concept of animal conservation was recast with the modern significance of bird protection and cultivation as the "protection of living things by human beings," a great change occurred in the hitherto equal relationship between birds and humans. In the process, it is clear that humans came to have an existence qualitatively higher than that of birds. And with the appearance of the modern view of the relationship between birds and humans the old discipline of natural history died. Most of the illustrations included within the present volume can in fact be considered the last surviving materials we have reflecting this now dead perception of living things when "birds and humans were equals."

In that sense, these beautiful bird illustrations can be considered a mirror in which we ourselves are reflected. And the reason that illustrations of animals are not merely a substitute for mounted specimens is found precisely there — because such illustrations make it possible for us to continually rediscover and reinterpret this kind of historical image of ourselves.

— HIROSHI ARAMATA

FANTASY, ADVENTURE, AND THE ORNITHOLOGIST

The Birds of America *was published from 1840 to 1844 in a "double-folio elephant-size" edition with a 66 cm x 1 m format; the prints were colored by hand. The work represents a very important event in the history of ornithology, but as a publication it was not successful: there were only 175 subscribers. The author was John James Audubon, born Jean Jacques Audubon, the illegitimate son of a French captain from Nantes who had settled in 1803 in New Orleans, at that time still called Nouvelle Orleans.*

At the time of the Bonaparte Consulate, Audubon was attending the Paris studio of the painter David and had started naturalistic observation with D'Orbigny. In America, he went into business, with little success, selling supplies to pioneers in Louisville, Kentucky, on the Ohio River – the "frontier" – and became involved in dubious mining enterprises. Most important, he traveled from end to end of the great country, which at that time did not yet extend from sea to sea. He traveled on foot or on horseback, sometimes in a canoe, together with his faithful dog, a long rifle, powder, lead, and a painter's box. The black Phoebe (page 177) is one of the birds this exceptional ornithologist portrayed.

For ornithology, this was a glorious time of discoveries, but the study of birds has a long history. "The priests of that temple [at Heliopolis, Egypt] date any written information to the time of a bird called the phoenix, a bird that is unique in all the world and that is burnt upon the altar of that temple every five hundred years, which is the duration of its life... This bird is often seen flying in that region, and it is no larger than an eagle. On its head is a crest of feathers, bigger than the peacock's, its neck is of a golden color like that of a stone windowsill polished shiny, its bill is indigo blue, its wings purple, and its tail has green, yellow, and red stripes. It is a wonderful bird to behold because it shines beautifully and gloriously." On page 87 is an illustration based on the phoenix from a Japanese text of the Edo period, but the quoted description is much older: it was written by the English knight John Mandeville, in his Travels, *or* Dissertation about the Most Marvellous and Remarkable Things that Exist in the World, *a text distributed in French shortly after the middle of the 14th*

century, then in Latin and English. Judging from the number of surviving manuscript copies, the work was well known, and it was repeatedly printed in the 16th century. The legend of the phoenix, however, is much older; as early as the 4th century, Christian allegorists were interpreting it as a prophecy of the Resurrection.

When, during the 18th century, the sage Samuel Johnson wrote that travels "hinder the impulse of imagination with the weight of reality," he was certainly not thinking of his fellow countryman of four centuries earlier, but he was perfectly correct: the natural sciences, ornithology among them, advanced at the same rate as geographic discoveries, which took place primarily by sea, and the blowing of ocean breezes set the sciences free from the mists of legends about the days "when men discoursed with birds."

Hasan ben Mohammed al Wazan al Zaiyati, a distinguished man of Granada, happened to belong to the generation that witnessed the fall of the last Islamic potentate in Spain. He migrated to Morocco, but while returning from a diplomatic mission he was captured at sea by Christian pirates and brought to Italy as a slave. Catechized and baptized by Pope Leo X, he lived in Italy during the third decade of the 16th century before somehow managing to return to the land of Islam. He is known to history as the Lion of Africa. Although neither a seafarer nor a discoverer, he belongs to that group of men who enlarged the European horizon; his Description of Africa and of the Remarkable Things Found There, *written in Italian, spread at first as a manuscript book among the educated and was then printed in the Ramusius books. It is considered to have been the summa of all that was known in Europe about Africa up to the early 19th century. The last pages concern animals. The Lion gives ample room to marvelous creatures — the public liked and expected such material — but he expressed certain reservations: "Several of our African historians say that the male of the eagle couples sometimes with a she-wolf and makes her pregnant, but she swells up so much that she cracks, and a dragon comes forth, with the bill and wings of a bird, the tail of a snake, and the feet of a wolf, and also the skin of a snake spotted with different colors; it has not* the strength to lift its eye lashes and lives in caves. But I have never seen it, nor have I met anyone who has seen it."

Jacques Cartier from Saint-Malo, one generation younger than the Lion of Africa, was a seafarer and discoverer: he ventured across the Atlantic three times, exploring west of Newfoundland and discovering the St. Lawrence and Canada (1534-1542). His reports give a taste of the sea and of the unknown unveiled: "These islands [the Bird Rocks] were more full of birds than a meadow is full of grass, and they had built their nests there, and there was especially a very large number of those birds that we call margaulx, which are white and bigger than geese, and they lived grouped in one place; in another place there were some isolated godetz, but on the beach there were some of these godetz and some big aporrath. "Margaulx are gannets, godetz are the auks with razor-shaped bills, and aporrath is the great auk, a bird that became extinct in 1844. In the few preceding pages Cartier gives probably its first description (and in his tale he implicitly gives also the cause of its future extinction): these birds are "black and white, with bills like crows: they live always on the water, nor can they fly high, as their wings are small, not larger than a half hand, with which however they can fly over the water surface as fast as the other birds fly in the air; they are extremely fat. We called them aporrath, and with them we loaded out two boats in less than half an hour, as we might have done with stones; therefore each ship salted four or five barrels of them, not including the birds we ate fresh." The great auk can be seen on page 25 together with the king penguin, in a picture from the early 19th-century edition, edited by Sonnini, of the Histoire naturelle by Buffon. At the time, the most stylistically efficient of all naturalists was already dead, but re-editions, integrations, supplements, and updatings of his work for a long time engaged many natural scientists and produced, as far as our subject is concerned, very valuable ornithologic pictures. Not many years after Cartier's voyages, while geographic discovery was still in its first stage, Pierre Bélon, a Frenchman, published the Histoire de la nature des oiseaux (1555), the first monograph about birds, and its xylographs illustrated two hundred species. In the Historia animalium of the encyclopaedic naturalist and physician Conrad Gesner from Zurich, which had been published a short time before (1551), even more species are illustrated. For about two centuries Gesner's work remained an undisputable reference point.

Let's open any naturalistic textbook of today. Birds are described as warm-blooded animals that reproduce through eggs, have a body covered with feathers, and have forward limbs transformed into wings. It is pointed out that, second only to mammals, they are the animals with the most developed intelligence. Some naturalists even maintain that the mental faculties of several birds rival those of the most intelligent mammals. Their biological activity seems to be accelerated: blood temperature is higher than in mammals, tissues are renovated more quickly, blood circulation and breathing are faster. As a consequence, birds consume a lot of energy, therefore they must feed much more and much more frequently than other animals. They devote to feeding all the time they do not spend sleeping and have a short life: the titmouse lives only one year, not many other birds live over three years (but the sparrow lives 18 years, the seagull 30, and the crow almost 70 years).

Nowadays all this is very well know. But the point on which to focus our attention is the number of species now known — over eight thousand — forty times the number described by Bélon. This increase of our knowledge is one of the results of the two centuries, the 18th and the 19th, to which the pictures of birds in this book belong. The universe of birds presented in this book reflects above all the fascination of uncontaminated spaces, the salty smell of the seas, the immense green of forests, the "fleuves impassibles," the tropical islands...

It was in the 18th century that exploration took on a different characteristic. The gracefully artificial attitude that we often attribute to the 18th century makes us forget many things: the period's curiosity and scientific bent, its desire to know all and catalog all. It is the century of encyclopedias (the English Chambers Encyclopaedia, 1728, and the Diderot and d'Alembert Encyclopédie, 1751); for natural history, it is the century of Linnaeus (and Buffon). From a certain moment of the 18th century no naval discovery expedition left harbor without a scientific team on board; the geographic-cartographic aim (and consequently the mathematical-astronomical one) came first because of its obvious practical results, but the scientific general staff always included a naturalist, accompanied by a painter. Bougainville, who started his voyage around the world in 1766, embarked Philibert Commerson, whom Voltaire would have liked to have as secretary and whose work on Mediterranean fish had been much appreciated by Linnaeus. (Commerson had an assistant, who waited upon him at table, carried his luggage during the scientific excursions on land, and in his spare time sorted out the collections. The Tahitians discovered that this assistant was a woman, Jeanne Baré, who was travelling in a man's clothes.) On departing for his first voyage (1768), Captain Cook was accompanied by Joseph Banks, a disciple of Linnaeus's, and for the documentation, by a draftsman and a painter. The unlucky La Pérouse (no one returned from his expedition, which departed in 1785) was accompanied by the naturalist La Martinière and, as painters, by the two Prévosts, uncle and nephew. The two Prévosts disappeared with the expedition, but not their material, which had been sent to France overland from Petropavlosk in the Kamchatka peninsula. The paintings made by the Prévosts in the course of the expedition also include some beautiful pictures of birds, but the general impression one receives is that the naturalists accompanying these expeditions were more interested in botany than in other branches of natural history. It is extraordinary how fascinating botany was to 18th-century people: Rousseau, "une loupe à la main, et mon Systema naturae [by Linnaeus] sous le bras," botanizing on the island of Saint-Pierre in the lake of Bienne (Biel, Switzerland), appears to be almost a symbol of the spirit of the time.

It was, however, a "philosophical" time. In his Voyage autour du monde, Louis-Antonine de Bougainville (1771), who had a supplemental edition of Diderot, writes: "It was not an uncommon sight, on our arrival, to see all the animals, up to that moment the only inhabitants of the island [one of the Maluinas, or Malvinas, or Falkland], draw near with no fear and do no other movements but those inspired by curiosity on contemplating an unknown reality. Birds let themselves be caught in our hands, some came to perch on the people that stood still: how true that man shows no sign of his ferocity on his face, a sign that would allow the weaker animals to recognize him, by pure instinct, as the being that feeds on their blood. This confidence did not last long: very soon they learned to mistrust their most cruel enemy."

To tell the truth, though unpleasant to admit, the ornithologist also made progress into his science with a gun. However, this progress was rather complicated. Those great, marvelous collections of ornithological pictures of the 18th, 19th, and even the early 20th century — this "lost form of art," that came to an end with photography — were created by the use of many different methods and very often with the contribution of different professional experiences. There were the artists on board the ships of the above-mentioned explorations, who worked "in the field," drawing or painting from life or portraying immediately birds captured or killed on purpose; there were the artists who took part later in the exclusively scientific expeditions organized by cultural institutions; and there were people who traveled in search of the various specimens, drew sketches, took notes, sent the animals to the taxidermist (or stuffed them themselves), and later availed themselves of specialized artists to portray their features. The materials collected in the course of the explorations ended up, except in some unlucky cases of shipwreck or other accidents with loss of the precious boxes (as did happen), in natural history museums. Other materials (hides or stuffed birds) found their way into private collections, and so collections of ornithological illustrations, even of exotic species, could be created after careful inspections of museums and private naturalistic collections. Briefly, the ornithologist and the artist could be either one person or two or more persons; usually the ornithologist was in the preeminent position (a situation that could and in fact did lead to difficult relationships, sometimes with unpleasant consequences).

The publishing of these pictures involved both technical problems requiring the intervention of specialized workers (engravers, lithographers) and economic problems. Most of the known collections of ornithological illustrations were the result of costly activities that went on for years. The publishing often took the form of separate volumes. Some of them were supported by public patronage (and political changes often left them unfinished), some by private patronage, others were partially or totally supported by sale. Twelve kings, eleven royal highnesses, sixteen dukes, thirty viscounts, and sixty-one barons were known to be among the subscribers to John Gould's works. However, the public was not all noblemen or scientific institutions: it was certainly composed of wealthy persons, for these were expensive books even when first published, but the good luck of some initiatives can be perceived sometimes as a matter of fashion. It is fascinating to observe how unexpected details of the time, scientific trends, artistic tastes and inclinations, cultural tendencies, social habits, are mirrored in the ornithological illustrations as in a crystal.

John James Audubon is perhaps the best example of the ornithologist painter. When Cuvier presented Audubon's Birds of America to the Academie des Sciences in Paris, he described it as "le plus magnifique monument que l'art ait jamais élevé à la nature." So, the two words that are the reading key of this book were authoritatively uttered for the ornithological illustrations: "nature" and "art." Gould, on the other hand, is the best example of another way of working: he watched, drew sketches, shot the birds to be studied, and left the artistic work to collaborators whom he had cleverly selected and whom he carefully directed. A remarkable collaborator of his was Edward Lear, best known today for his place in Victorian literature thanks to his popular "nonsense verses." A self-taught naturalist, Lear had started at the age of nineteen to paint parrots from life, and the Viscount of Derby engaged him to portray the exotic animals of the menagerie he had in his country possessions. The ornithologists of the time criticized Lear because he painted the "portrait" of a bird instead of stressing the general characteristics of the species, the "type"; this is a very subtle doctrinal detail. However, John Gould's most important collaborator was a woman called Elisabeth, who was both painter and wife to him for eighteen years, gave him six children, and died at the age of thirty-seven. Among other things, John and Elisabeth Gould illustrated one of Darwin's

naturalistic reports after his famous tour around the world on H.M.S. Beagle; it included the Galapagos chaffinch, which was one of the starting points of meditation for the elaboration of his evolution principles. Many beautiful pictures of birds were painted after the publication of On the Origin of Species, but for the world of natural history no more important event had probably ever taken place than the journey of the Beagle.

Ostriches, penguins, storm petrels, pelicans, storks, flamingoes, swans, and ducks

The birds on the following pages belong to twelve different orders and twenty-seven families. The largest groups are represented by the Anseriformes (ducks, geese, and swans), the Ciconiiformes, and the Procellariiformes. At the opposite end are orders that include very few species but are very well known and largely diffused.

All these birds are characterized by a very high degree of specialization: the Tinamiformes are typical land birds that, however, can still fly: ostriches, emus, nandus, and kiwis, on the contrary, are so well adapted to life on land that they have even lost their wings. Penguins have so well adapted to life in the sea that they have lost the capacity to fly and have even modified the structural characteristics of the feathers that protect them, so that their feathers look almost like hairs. Loons, grebes, and Procellariiformes, also well adapted to live permanently on the water, have kept and sometimes wonderfully developed the capacity to fly, but they have lost completely or almost completely the capacity of walking on land. Finally, Pelecaniformes, Ciconiiformes, and Anseriformes are typically aquatic birds that have kept the capacity to both fly and walk on land.

*Above, nandu and Darwin's nandu
(*Rhea americana *and*
Pterocnemia pennata,
*Rheiformes, Rheidae), from
Groenvold and Kirke, 1915-17 (26).
Left, nandu. Below, ostrich
(*Struthio camelus,
*Struthioniformes, Struthionidae),
from Cuvier, 1836-49 (9).*

Top, double-wattled cassowary (Casuarius casuarius,
Casuariiformes, Casuariidae), from D'Orbigny, 1837 (15).
Above, emu (Dromaius novaehollandiae,
Casuariiformes, Casuariidae), from Gould, 1840-48 (21).
Right, brown kiwi (Apteriyx australis, Apterygiformes,
Apterygidae), from Gould, 1840-48 (21).

*Andean tinamou (*Nothoprocta pentlandii, *Tinamiformes, Tinamidae), from Groenvold and Kirke, 1915-17 (26).*

*Above, brown tinamou (*Crypturellus obsoletus, *Tinamiformes, Tinamidae), from Temminck and Laugier de Chartrouse, 1820-39 (48). Below, solitary tinamou (*Tinamus solitarius, *Tinamiformes, Tinamidae), from Groenvold and Kirke, 1915-17 (26).*

Above, red-winged tinamou (Rhynchotus rufescens, Tinamiformes, Tinamidae), from Temminck and Laugier de Chartrouse, 1820-39 (48). Below, nestling and eggs, from Zoological Society of London, 1870 (51).

Above, elegant crested tinamou and dwarf tinamou (Endromia elegans and Taomiscus nanus, Tinamiformes, Tinamidae), from Groenvold and Kirke, 1915-17 (26). Top right, tataupa tinamou (Crypturellus tataupa, Tinamiformes, Tinamidae), from Temminck and Laugier de Chartrouse, 1820-39 (48).

Left, jackass penguin (Spheniscus demersus, Sphenisciformes, Spheniscidae), from Cuvier, 1836-49 (9). Below, rockhopper penguin (Eudyptes crestatus, Sphenisciformes, Spheniscidae), from D'Orbigny, 1837 (15).

Below, king penguin (Aptenodytes patagoncia, Sphenisciformes, Spheniscidae), together with the now extinct great auk (Pinguinus impennis), from Buffon, 1799-1808 (4).

Above, little penguin (Eudyptula minor, Sphenisciformes, Spheniscidae), from Zoological Society of London, 1870 (51).

Left, great northern diver (Gavia immer, Gaviiformes, Gaviidae), from Cuvier, 1836-49 (9). Below, red-throated diver (Gavia stellata, Gaviiformes, Gaviidae), from Donovan, 1794-1819 (13).

Above, great grebe (Podiceps major, Podicipediformes, Podicipedidae), from Groenvold and Kirke, 1915-17 (26). Left, great crested grebe (Podiceps cristatus, Podicipediformes, Podicipedidae), from Buffon, 1853-57 (5).

Short tailed albatross (Diomedea albatrus, Procellariiformes, Diomedeidae), from Temminck and Laugier de Chartrouse, 1820-39 (48).

Below, sooty albatross (Phoebetria fusca, Procellariiformes, Diomedeidae), from Temminck and Laugier de Chartrouse, 1820-39 (48). Right, wandering albatross (Diomedea exulans, Procellariiformes, Diomedeidae), from Cuvier, 1836-49 (9).

Left, black-browed albatross (Diomedea melanophrys, Procellariiformes, Diomedeidae), from Temminck and Laugier de Chartrouse, 1820-39 (48). Above, yellow-nosed albatross (Diomedea chlororhynchos, Procellariiformes, Diomedeidae), from Temminck and Laugier de Chartrouse, 1820-39 (48).

*White-faced shearwater
(Calonectris leucomelas,
Procellariiformes, Procellariidae),
from Temminck and Laugier de
Chartrouse, 1820-39 (48).*

*Black-capped petrel (Pterodroma
hasitata, Procellariiformes,
Procellariidae), from Temminck and
Laugier de Chartrouse, 1820-39
(48).*

*Broad-billed prion (Pachyptila
vittata, Procellariiformes,
Procellariidae), from Temminck and
Laugier de Chartrouse, 1820-39
(48).*

*Pintado petrel (Daption capense,
Procellariiformes, Procellariidae),
from Cuvier, 1836-49 (9).*

Above, fork-tailed storm petrel (Oceanodroma furcata, Procellariiformes, Hydrobatidae), from De Kay, 1844 (11). Below, Wilson's petrel (Oceanites oceanicus, Procellariiformes, Hydrobatidae), from De Kay, 1844 (11). Below left, fairy prion (Pachyptila turtur, Procellariiformes, Hydrobatidae), from Smith, 1838-49 (45).

Top, red-billed tropic bird (Phaeton aethereus, Pelecaniformes, Phaetontidae), from Leach, 1814-17 (27). Center, white-tailed tropic bird (Phaeton lepturus, Pelecaniformes, Phaetontidae), from Cuvier, 1836-49 (9). Below, brown pelican (Pelecanus occidentalis, Pelecaniformes, Pelecanidae), from Zoological Society of London, 1870 (51).

*Above right, Australian pelican (*Pelecanus conspicillatus, *Pelecaniformes, Pelecanidae), from Temminck and Laugier de Chartrouse, 1820-39 (48). Above and right, white pelican (*Pelecanus onocrotalus, *Pelecaniformes, Pelecanidae), from Bree, 1859-63 (3), and from Buffon, 1853-57 (5).*

Der Dölpel

M. Catesby ad viv delin.

C. P. S. C. Majestatis
N°. 74 IV ter Thail.

J. M. Seligmann excud.

Anseri baffano affinis fufca avis
Sula leucogaster

Le Fou.

*Brown booby (*Sula leucogaster,
*Pelecaniformes, Sulidae), from Catesby,
1754 (6).*

Below left, Indian darter (Anhinga melanogaster, Pelecaniformes, Anhingidae), from Temminck and Laugier de Chartrouse, 1820-39 (48). Below right, shag (Phalacrocorax aristotelis, Pelecaniformes, Phalacrocoracidae), from Temminck and Laugier de Chartrouse, 1820-39 (48).

Left, common cormorant (Phalacrocorax carbo, Pelecaniformes, Phalacrocoracidae), from Leach, 1814-17 (27). Above, Ascension frigate bird (Fregata aquila, Pelecaniformes, Fregatidae), from Buffon, 1853-57 (5).

*Left, little egret (*Egretta garzetta, *Ciconiiformes, Ardeidae), from Donovan, 1794-1819 (13). Below left, purple heron (*Ardea purpurea, *Ciconiiformes, Ardeidae), from D'Orbigny, 1837 (15). Below right, grey heron (*Ardea cinerea, *Ciconiiformes, Ardeidae), from Donovan, 1794-1819 (13).*

Top left, whistling heron (Syrigma sibilator, Ciconiiformes, Ardeidae), from Temminck and Laugier de Chartrouse, 1820-39 (48). Top right, rufescent tiger heron (Tigrisoma lineatum, Ciconiiformes, Ardeidae), from Temminck and Laugier de Chartrouse, 1820-39 (48). Above, Japanese night heron (Gorsachius goisagi, Ciconiiformes, Ardeidae), from Temminck and Laugier de Chartrouse, 1820-39 (48). Right, boat-billed heron (Cochlearius cochlearius, Ciconiiformes, Cochleariidae), from Cuvier, 1836-49 (9).

Above, white stork (Ciconia ciconia, Ciconiiformes, Ciconiidae), from Cuvier, 1836-49 (9). Above right, hammerkop (Scopus umbretta, Ciconiiformes, Scopidae), from Cuvier, 1836-49 (9). Right, Asian open-bill stork (Anastomus oscitans, Ciconiiformes, Ciconiidae), from Cuvier, 1836-49 (9). Below, whaleheaded stork (Balaeniceps rex, Ciconiiformes, Balaenicipitidae), from Wolf, 1861-67 (50).

*Lesser adjutant stork
(Leptoptilos javanicus,
Ciconiiformes, Ciconiidae),
from Temminck and Laugier de
Chartrouse, 1820-39 (48).*

*African open-bill stork
(Anastomus lamelligerus,
Ciconiiformes, Ciconiidae),
from Temminck and Laugier de
Chartrouse, 1820-39 (48).*

*Saddle-bill stork
(Ephippiorhynchus
senegalensis, Ciconiiformes,
Ciconiidae), from Cuvier, 1836-
49 (9).*

*Sacred ibis (Threeskiornis aethiopicus,
Threskiornithidae, Ciconiidae), from Pouchet, 1841
(42).*

Three representations of the Japanese crested ibis (Nipponia nippon, Ciconiiformes, Threskiornithidae), from Temminck and Laugier de Chartrouse, 1820-39 (48) and from David, 1877 (10).

Below left, black ibis (Pseudibis papillosa, Ciconiiformes, Threskiornithidae), from Temminck and Laugier de Chartrouse, 1820-39 (48). Below right, Oriental ibis (Threskiornis melanocephalus, Ciconiiformes, Threskiornithidae), from Temminck and Laugier de Chartrouse, 1820-39 (48).

Left, glossy ibis (Plegadis falcinellus, Ciconiiformes, Threskiornithidae), from Donovan, 1794-1819 (13). Above, buff-necked ibis (Theristicus caudatus, Ciconiiformes, Threskiornithidae), from Temminck and Laugier de Chartrouse, 1820-39 (48).

Above, white spoonbill (Platalea leucorodia, Ciconiiformes, Threskiornithidae), from Cuvier, 1836-49 (9). Right, beaks, from Takagi, 1852 (47). Right and below, greater flamingo (Phoenicopterus ruber, Phoenicopteriformes, Phoenicopteridae), from Buffon, 1853-57 (5), and from Cuvier, 1836-49 (9).

Above left, lesser flamingo (Phoeniconaias minor, Phoenicopteriformes, Phoenicopteridae), from Temminck and Laugier de Chartrouse, 1820-39 (48). Above, horned screamer (Anhima cornuta, Anseriformes, Anhimidae), from D'Orbigny, 1873 (15). Below left, Andean flamingo (Phoenicoparrus andinus, Phoenicopteriformes, Phoenicopteridae), from Pouchet, 1841 (42). Left, northern screamer (Chauna chavaria, Anseriformes, Anhimidae), from Temminck and Laugier de Chartrouse, 1820-39 (48).

Left, mute swan (Cygnus olor, Anseriformes, Anatidae), from Buffon, 1853-57 (5). Below, black-necked swan (Cygnus melanocoryphus, Anseriformes, Anatidae), from Gay, 1844-71 (19).

Left and above, mallards (Anas platyrhynchos, Anseriformes, Anatidae), from Buffon 1853-57 (5) and Cuvier, 1836-49 (9).

Above, white-fronted goose (Anser albifrons, Anseriformes, Anatidae), from Donovan, 1794-1819 (13). Below, Egyptian goose (Alopochen aegyptiacus, Anseriformes, Anatidae), from Donovan, 1794-1819 (13).

Top, green-winged teal (Anas crecca, Anseriformes, Anatidae), from Cuvier, 1836-49 (9), and hooded merganser (Mergus cucullatus, Anseriformes, Anatidae), from Cuvier, 1836-49 (9).

Top, Mandarin duck (Aix galericulata, *Anseriformes, Anatidae), from D'Orbigny, 1837 (15). Center, musk duck (Biziura lobata, Anseriformes, Anatidae), from Temminck and Laugier de Chartrouse, 1820-39 (48). Bottom, long-tailed duck (Clangula hyemalis, Anseriformes, Anatidae), from Donovan, 1794-1819 (13).*

Below left, common shoveler (Anas clypeata, Anseriformes, Anatidae), from Cuvier, 1836-49 (9). Below right, common scoter (Melanitta nigra, Anseriformes, Anatidae), from Cuvier, 1836-49 (9). Center left, common shelduck (Tadorna tadorna, Anseriformes, Anatidae), from Cuvier, 1836-49 (9).

Americanische Ente mit breitem Schnabel.   Tab. XCII

Above, king eidor (Somateria spectabilis, Anseriformes, Anatidae), from Cuvier, 1836-49 (9). Right, common shoveler (Anas clypeata, Anseriformes, Anatidae), from Catesby, 1754 (6).

In the field and in the naturalist's studio: the labors involved in cataloging the new

The illustrations of the short tailed albatross, the shag, and the lesser flamingo (pages 27, 34, and 42), and the descriptions of many more species in this chapter and in the following ones are the result of the ambitious project suggested by the Dutch patrician Coenraad Jacob Temminck to his friend the baron Meiffren Laugier de Chartrouse in January 1820 in Paris. Both were keen ornithologists and owned large collections of stuffed exotic birds; both had the idea to add to the 973 colored plates of birds (the *Planches Enluminées*) published by Edmé Louis Daubenton in the years 1765-1783 under the patronage of the famous Buffon. They wanted to assemble all the new bird species that the naval expeditions and geographic explorations promoted by the great European powers had brought back to the various museums and to the natural history laboratories during the first two decades of the century.

On September 1, 1820, the *Nouveau recueil de planches coloriées* began. The work was going to consist of successive issues of in-folio plates followed by the relevant text, which would be bound into several volumes at the end of publication; it addressed not only the specialist and the libraries of the most important museums, but also an educated and (above all) wealthy public that appreciated beauty. The artists chosen to portray the subjects were two Frenchmen, Jean-Gabriel Prête (about 1800-1840) and Nicolas Huet (1770-1830), two very well known painters of animal subjects. Very soon they started gathering new ornithological subjects to be portrayed: Brazilian birds brought back by the South American expedition of Prince Maximilian of Wied; sea birds of the English, French, and Dutch naval expeditions in the Australian seas; birds from South-Eastern Asia, brought back by the Dutch East India Company, which at the time was patronizing systematic researches into the animal and vegetable kingdoms all over the colonies. Temminck, in addi-

tion to his own and Laugier's collections, was able to examine the large collections of the king of France in Paris, of the British Crown in London, and the Royal Museums of Vienna and Berlin. From the reports written by naturalist travelers, he could obtain and compare important information concerning the habits of birds in nature. A very interesting chapter, because it describes birds that at the time were little known in Europe, is the one Temminck dedicates to the new species of storm-petrels and albatrosses, which is worth reading because of its lively style: "These birds are usually of a strong build, adapted to fly long distances. Petrels and albatrosses have tapering, slender wings; their muscles end with strong tendons which allow them to fly enormous distances on the open sea; their widely webbed feet make resting on the waves easier; their sharp sight makes the destiny of the fish, of which they are greedy, unavoidable: they don't grab them by plunging into the water but while flying over the surface. Seafarers often come across these birds at incredible distances from the dry land and they are seldom seen to fly beyond the boundaries of the areas where they usually live. They always glide as they are flying; if sometimes they flutter their wings, this has the only purpose of rising more rapidly; more often their out-spread wings form a hollow underneath; apparently they do not vibrate at all, no matter how many different positions the animal takes, both as it follows the ripples of the waves while flying, skimming the surface of the water, and as it makes large turns, while rising, around ships or floating cetaceans indicating the place where they can feed. After resting on the water surface, albatrosses must make a big effort to take flight; to do this, they must be urged by some pressing circumstance: in this case we can see them run on the water surface for a distance of over 40–60 arm-lengths before they can take flight. By swimming, they can move away quickly. In flight, they can rise high very easily, turning over abruptly with the help of their tail and can fly also against the strongest wind without apparently slowing down their motion and without moving their wings with any perceptible flutter. All those who have seen them agree on emphasizing the extraordinary strength of their flight; petrels have been seen to fly for days on end. After landing on the water surface, they keep their wings spread out for a short time; when they are folded along their bodies, they spoil the elegance of their shapes, because they form a protuberance toward the end of the body.''

Temminck and Laugier's work, really a colossal one, came to an end only sixteen years later, in 1836; in the last volume, taking leave from his public, Temminck said good-bye to the supporters of his publishing efforts with these words: ''Now we must only thank the [French] government, whose efficient protection never stopped patronizing this work, although under three different kings. Though I am personally a stranger to this French country that encourages so liberally sciences and arts, I consider myself a lucky man, and I am proud of having accomplished such an enormous undertaking without ever meeting either the faintest difficulty of publication or experiencing the disagreements of bitter criticism, suggested by ill-will or generated by envy. I hope this addition to Buffon's works is not judged to be too much below the great model that I have taken the liberty to follow as a guide!''

Equally enterprising as a ''publisher'' of natural history was the Englishman Mark Catesby, who had lived many years before (1683-1749), and who made the engravings, water-colored by hand, of a brown booby and of a common shoveler (pages 33 and 46). Very interested in botany, Catesby moved from Norfolk, England, his birthplace, to London, where a ''gardeners' society'' was flourishing. Later on, in 1710, he decided to join his married sister, who resided in the English colony of Virginia in the New World. On returning to England in 1715, he brought back a large collection of plants and seeds that immediately raised the interest of certain wealthy English collectors and keen botanists, among whom was Sir Hans Sloane. The collectors decided to promote another journey to America, provided they could have, as compensation, seeds and plants to be acclimatized in their gardens, and birds, insects, shells, and corals for their scientific collections. To that end Catesby remained in Carolina until 1726 and became not only a ''curiosity'' collector but also a careful researcher of natural history and an expert of the North American fauna and flora, at the time still unknown in Europe. On returning to England he decided to write a book about his explorations in America, and a first volume was published in 1731 with the title *The Natural History of Carolina, Florida and the Bahama Islands, containing the figures of Birds, beasts, fishes, serpents, insects and plants.* In addition to a map of the explored regions, the book also contained several water-colored engravings of plants, birds, mammals, reptiles, and fish. To cut down the expenses of the graphic part, which was quite necessary, Catesby decided to make the preliminary drawings and etch them in the copper plates by himself. Therefore he took engraving lessons from Joseph Goupy (1689-1763), at the time the best copper-plate engraver. His work was a great success, and in 1733 Catesby's scientific competence was rewarded by election to *Fellow* of the Royal Society. To avoid wasting plates, Catesby decided to etch on each plate the chosen animal together with parts of plants, such as leaves, flowers, and fruits, that could be very clearly identifiable as species. This matching, sometimes slightly *naif*, resulted in a very pleasant page, and it can be considered as the first model for books portraying animals in their natural habitat.

Sparrow hawks, eagles, cocks, pheasants, and cranes

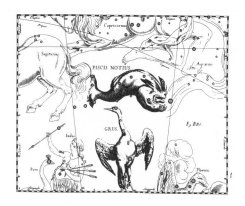

The birds described in this chapter fall into three separate orders: *Falconiformes, Galliformes, and Gruiformes. The general appearance of the birds in the first two orders is rather homogeneous and easily identifiable: all Falconiformes, large, small, or very small, have the typical appearance of diurnal predatory birds, with a curved bill and claws suited to grabbing; all Galliformes have more or less the appearance of a "chicken" with a typical inclination to walking on land and scratching about in search of food. However, after a more careful examination, it is possible to notice that, whereas the uniformity of Galliformes is true (it derives from a common origin in a not very remote time), the uniformity of Falconiformes is, at least partially, fictitious: the vultures of the New World are not closely related to those of the Old World, and the true hawks constitute another separate small group. A few authors have even suggested the creation of three separate orders.*

Gruiformes are divided into twelve separate families that include birds rather different from one another. The most important and numerous ones, in addition to the family of the proper cranes (Gruidae family) and bustards (Otididae family), are the Rallidae and the coturnix *genus, or three-dactyl quails. The other families are very small and include a few species whose precise systematic positioning often represents a puzzle.*

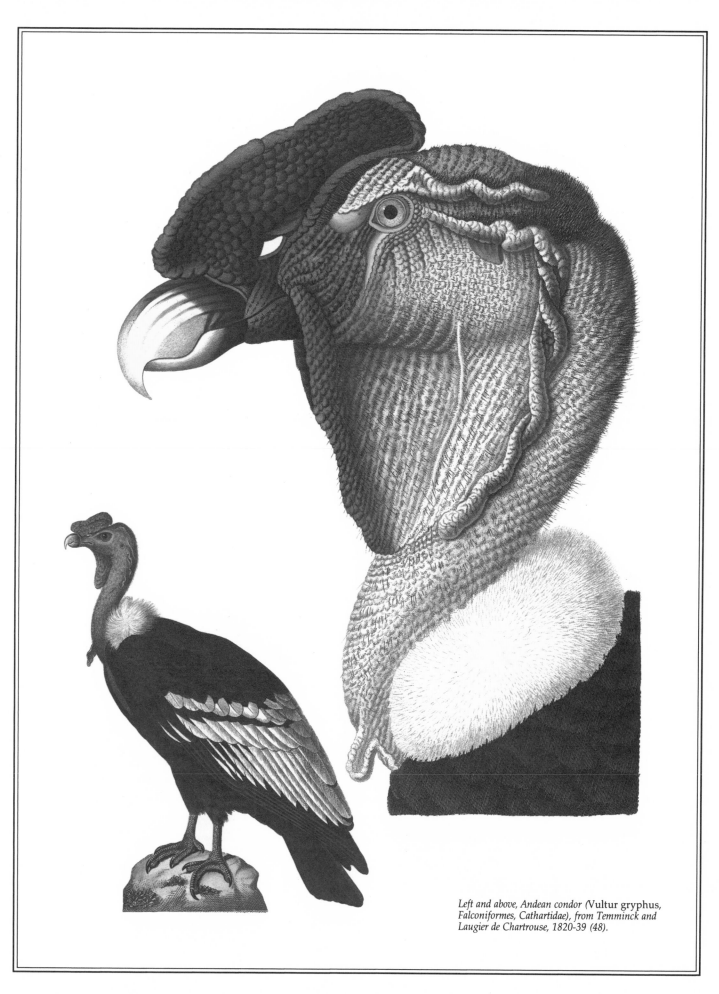

*Left and above, Andean condor (Vultur gryphus,
Falconiformes, Cathartidae), from Temminck and
Laugier de Chartrouse, 1820-39 (48).*

51

*Turkey vulture (*Cathartes aura, *Falconiformes, Cathartidae), from Vieillot, 1807 (49).*

*California condor (*Gymnogyps californianus, *Falconiformes, Cathartidae), from Temminck and Laugier de Chartrouse, 1820-39 (48).*

*Below left, king vulture (*Sarcoramphus papa, *Falconiformes, Cathartidae), from D'Orbigny, 1837 (15). Below, Andean condor (*Vultur gryphus, *Falconiformes, Cathartidae), from Temminck and Laugier de Chartrouse, 1820-39 (48).*

Top left and left, Himalayan griffon (Gyps himalayensis, Falconiformes, Accipitridae), from Gray, 1830-34 (25). The heads at left: top, European black vulture (Aegypius monachus), *and bottom, Asiatic king vulture* (Aegypius calvus), *both Falconiformes, Accipitridae, from Gray, 1830-34 (25).*

Above left, griffon vulture (Gyps fulvus, Falconiformes, Accipitridae), from Gray, 1830-34 (25). Top right, Indian griffon (Gyps indicus, Falconiformes, Accipitridae), from Temminck and Laugier de Chartrouse, 1820-39 (48). Above right, white-headed vulture (Aegypius occipitailis, Falconiformes, Accipitridae), from Temminck and Laugier de Chartrouse, 1820-39 (48).

Indian black eagle (Ictinaetus malayensis, Falconiformes, Accipitridae), from Temminck and Laugier de Chartrouse, 1820-39 (48).

Harpy eagle (Harpja harpyja, Falconiformes, Accipitridae), from Temminck and Laugier de Chartrouse, 1820-39 (48).

Below left, white-bellied sea eagle (Haliaetus leucogaster, Falconiformes, Accipitridae), from Temminck and Laugier de Chartrouse, 1820-39 (48). Below right, golden eagle (Aquila chrysaetos, Falconiformes, Accipitridae), from Cuvier, 1836-49 (9).

Left, tawny eagle (Aquila rapax, Falconiformes, Accipitridae), from Temminck and Laugier de Chartrouse, 1820-39 (48). Center, American bald eagle (Haliaetus leucocephalus, Falconiformes, Accipitridae), from Vieillot, 1807 (49). Top, lammergeier (Gypaetus barbatus, Falconiformes, Accipitridae), from Temminck and Laugier de Chartrouse, 1820-39 (48).

Above, imperial eagle (Aquila heliaca, Falconiformes, Accipitridae), from D'Orbigny, 1837 (15). Below, martial eagle (Poleametus bellicosus, Falconiformes, Accipitridae), from Smith, 1838-49 (45).

Top right, lammergeier (Gypaetus barbatus, Falconiformes, Accipitridae), from Cuvier, 1836-49 (9). Left, white-tailed sea eagle (Haliaetus albicilla, Falconiformes, Accipitridae), from Susemihl, 1839-51 (46).

Above left, Verreaux eagle (Aquila verreauxii, Falconiformes, Accipitridae), from Lesson, 1830-32 (30). Left, greater spotted eagle (Aquila clanga, Falconiformes, Accipitridae), from Gray, 1830-34 (25). Above, Steller's sea eagle (Haliaetus pelagicus, Falconiformes, Accipitridae), from Temminck and Laugier de Chartrouse, 1820-39 (48).

*Below left, black hawk eagle (*Spizaetus tyrannus, *Falconiformes, Accipitridae), from Temminck and Laugier de Chartrouse, 1820-39 (48). Below right, Oriental honey buzzard (*Pernis ptilorhynchus, *Falconiformes, Accipitridae), from Temminck and Laugier de Chartrouse, 1820-39 (48).*

*Above left and right, African goshawk (*Accipiter tachiro, *Falconiformes, Accipitridae), from Temminck and Laugier de Chartrouse, 1820-39 (48).*

Below left, European sparrow hawk (Accipiter nisus, Falconiformes, Accipitridae), from Buffon, 1853-57 (5).

Above left, northern goshawk (Accipiter gentilis, Falconiformes, Accipitridae). Above right, booted eagle (Hieraetus pennatus, Falconiformes, Accipitridae), both from Temminck and Laugier de Chartrouse, 1820-39 (48).

Right, great black hawk (Buteogallus urubitinga, Falconiformes, Accipitridae). Below, black-faced hawk (Leucopternis melanops, Falconiformes, Accipitridae), both from Temminck and Laugier de Chartrouse, 1820-39 (48).

Above, rufous-winged buzzard eagle (Butastur liventer, Falconiformes, Accipitridae), from Temminck and Laugier de Chartrouse, 1820-39 (48). Below, crowned solitary eagle (Harpyhaliaetus coronatus, Falconiformes, Accipitridae), from Temminck and Laugier de Chartrouse, 1820-39 (48).

*Below right, Harris's hawk (*Parabuteo
unicinctus, *Falconiformes, Accipitridae), from
Buffon, 1853-57 (5).*

*Above left, large-billed hawk (*Buteo magnirostris,
*Falconiformes, Accipitridae), from Temminck and Laugier de
Chartrouse, 1820-39 (48). Above right, white-necked hawk
(*Leucopternis lacernulata, *Falconiformes, Accipitridae), from
Temminck and Laugier de Chartrouse, 1820-39 (48).*

*Below left, plumbeous kite (*Ictinia plumbea, *Falconiformes, Accipitridae). Below right and bottom right, hooked-billed kite (*Chondrohierax uncinatus, *Falconiformes, Accipitridae). Bottom left, slender-billed kite (*Rostrhamus hamatus, *Falconiformes, Accipitridae), all from Temminck and Laugier de Chartrouse, 1820-39 (48).*

Below left, gray-headed kite (Leptodon cayanensis, Falconiformes, Accipitridae), from Temminck and Laugier de Chartrouse, 1820-39 (48). Below, white-tailed kite (Elanus leucurus, Falconiformes, Accipitridae), from Gay, 1844-71 (19).

Above, double-toothed kite, and right, beak of double-toothed kite (Harpagus bidentatus, Falconiformes, Accipitridae), from Temminck and Laugier de Chartrouse, 1820-39 (48).

Black harrier (Circus maurus, *Falconiformes, Accipitridae), from Temminck and Laugier de Chartrouse, 1820-39 (48).*

Barred forest falcon (Micrastur ruficollis, *Falconiformes, Falconidae), from Temminck and Laugier de Chartrouse, 1820-39 (48).*

Reunion marsh harrier (Circus aeruginosus maillardi, *Falconiformes, Accipitridae), from Temminck and Laugier de Chartrouse, 1820-39 (48).*

Osprey *(Pandion haliaetus, Falconiformes, Accipitridae), from Temminck and Laugier de Chartrouse, 1820-39 (48).*

*Right, osprey (Pandion haliaetus,
Falconiformes, Accipitridae), from Donovan,
1794-1819 (13). Below, common caracara
(Polyborus plancus, Falconiformes,
Accipitridae), from Gay, 1844-71 (19).*

*Above, common kestrel (*Falco tinnunculus, *Falconiformes, Falconidae), from Mayer, 1853-57 (36). Below, lesser kestrel (*Falco naumanni, *Falconiformes, Falconidae), from Mayer, 1853-57 (36).*

Lanner falcon (Falco biarmicus, Falconiformes, Falconidae), from Temminck and Laugier de Chartrouse, 1820-39 (48).

European hobby (Falco subbuteo, Falconiformes, Falconidae), from Donovan, 1794-1819 (13).

Secretary bird (Sagittarius serpentarius, Falconiformes, Falconidae), from Pouchet, 1841 (42).

Below left, rock ptarmigan (Lagopus mutus, Galliformes, Tetraonidae), from Gaimard, 1838-52 (18). Right, crested bobwhite (Colinus cristatus, Galliformes, Phasianidae), from Cuvier, 1836-49 (9). Below right, willow/red grouse (Lagopus lagopus, Galliformes, Tetraonidae), from Gaimard, 1838-52 (18).

Left, black grouse (Tetrao tetrix, Galliformes, Tetraonidae), from Donovan, 1794-1819 (13). Right, capercaille (Tetrao urogallus, Galliformes, Tetraonidae), from Donovan, 1794-1819 (13).

Top left, common scrub hen (Megapodius freycinet, Galliformes, Megapodiidae), from Temminck and Laugier de Chartrouse, 1820-39 (48). Top right, razor-billed curassow (Crax mitu, Galliformes, Cracidae), from Temminck and Laugier de Chartrouse, 1820-39 (48). Right, rufous-vented chachalaca (Ortalis ruficauda, Galliformes, Cracidae), from Groenvold and Kirke, 1915-17 (26).

Left, great curassow (Crax rubra, Galliformes, Cracidae), from Cuvier, 1836-49 (9). Right, northern helmeted curassow (Crax pauxi, Galliformes, Cracidae), from Cuvier, 1836-49 (9).

White-crested guan (Penelope pileata, Galliformes, Cracidae), from Des Murs, 1845-49 (12).

71

Top, black-breasted quail (Coturnix coromandelica, Galliformes, Phasianidae), from Temminck and Laugier de Chartrouse, 1820-39 (48). Above, spot-winged wood quail (Odontophorus capueira, Galliformes, Phasianidae), from Groenvold and Kirke, 1915-17 (26). Left, California quail, (Lophortyx californica, Galliformes, Phasianidae), from Lesson, 1830-32 (30).

Left, Madagascar partridge (Margaroperdix madagarensis, Galliformes, Phasianidae), from Temminck and Laugier de Chartrouse, 1820-39 (48). Right, crested wood partridge (Rollulus rouloul, Galliformes, Phasianidae), from Temminck and Laugier de Chartrouse, 1820-39 (48).

Below, left and right, double-spurred francolin (Francolinus bicalcaratus, Galliformes, Phasianidae), from Pennant, 1790 (40).

*Above, Blyth's tragopan (*Tragopan blythii, *Galliformes, Phasianidae), from Zoological Society of London, 1870 (51). Right, satyr tragopan (*Tragopan satyra, *Galliformes, Phasianidae), from Temminck and Laugier de Chartrouse, 1820-39 (48).*

*Satyr tragopan (Tragopan satyra,
Galliformes, Phasianidae), from
Pennant 1798-1800 (41).*

Left and right, Indian grey francolin (Francolinus pondicerianus, Galliformes, Phasianidae), from Temminck and Laugier de Chartrouse, 1820-39 (48).

Below, snow partridge (Lerwa lerwa, Galliformes, Phasianidae), from David, 1877 (10).

Sand partridge (Ammoperdix hayi, Galliformes, Phasianidae), from Temminck and Laugier de Chartrouse, 1820-39 (48).

Left and below, grey jungle fowl (Gallus sonneratii, Galliformes, Phasianidae), from Temminck and Laugier de Chartrouse, 1820-39 (48). Bottom, green jungle fowl (Gallus varius, Galliformes, Phasianidae), from Temminck and Laugier de Chartrouse, 1820-39 (48).

Top, red jungle fowl (Gallus
gallus, Galliformes, Phasianidae),
from Temminck and Laugier de
Chartrouse, 1820-39 (48). Above,
Ceylon jungle fowl (Gallus
lafayettei, Galliformes,
Phasianidae), from Des Murs,
1845-49 (12).

Below left and right, Himalayan monal pheasant (Lophophorus impeyanus, Galliformes, Phasianidae), from Temminck and Laugier de Chartrouse, 1820-39 (48).

Below, Chinese monal pheasant (Lophophorus lhuysii, Galliformes, Phasianidae), from Zoological Society of London, 1870 (51).

Above, Sclater's monal pheasant (Lophophorus sclateri, Galliformes, Phasianidae), from Zoological Society of London, 1870 (51). Left, Swinhoe's pheasant (Lophura swinhoii, Galliformes, Phasianidae), from David, 1877 (10).

*Above, turkey (*Meleagris gallopavo, *Galliformes, Phasianidae) and helmeted guinea fowl (*Numida meleagris, *Galliformes, Numididae) both from Buffon, 1853-57 (5). Right, ocellated turkey (*Agriocharis ocellata, *Galliformes, Phasianidae), from Temminck and Laugier de Chartrouse, 1820-39 (48).*

*Below, Elliot's pheasant (*Syrmaticus ellioti, *Galliformes, Phasianidae), from David, 1877 (10). Bottom, blue eared pheasant (*Crossoptilon auritum, *Galliformes, Phasianidae), from David, 1877 (10).*

82

Below and bottom (adult male), copper pheasant
*(*Syrmaticus soemmerringi, *Galliformes, Phasianidae),*
from Temminck and Laugier de Chartrouse, 1820-39 (48).

Above, brown eared pheasant
*(*Crossoptilon mantchuricum, *Galliformes,*
Phasianidae), from David, 1877 (10).

Top right, Reeve's pheasant (Syrmaticus reevesii, Galliformes, Phasianidae), from Temminck and Laugier de Chartrouse, 1820-39 (48). Right, Japanese pheasant (Phasianus versicolor, Galliformes, Phasianidae), from Temminck and Laugier de Chartrouse, 1820-39 (48).

*Above and right, blood pheasant (*Ithaginis cruentus, *Galliformes, Phasianidae), from David, 1877 (10).*

Great argus pheasant (Argusianus argus, Galliformes, Phasianidae), from D'Orbigny, 1837 (15).

Below, Lady Amherst's pheasant
(Crysolophus amherstiae,
Galliformes, Phasianidae), from David,
1877 (10).

Above, golden pheasant (Chrysolophus pictus,
Galliformes, Phasianidae), from Buffon, 1853-57
(5). Right, imaginary pheasant, from Takagi, 19th
century (47).

Right, common peafowl (Pavo cristatus, Galliformes, Phasianidae), from Buffon, 1853-57 (5). Below, Burmese peacock pheasant (Polyplectron bicalcaratum, Galliformes, Phasianidae), from Gray, 1830-34 (25).

*Top, Sumatran peacock pheasant (*Polyplectron chalcurum,
*Galliformes, Phasianidae). Center, Rothschild's peacock pheasant
(*Polyplectron inopinatum, *Galliformes, Phasianidae). Above,
Palawan peacock pheasant (*Polyplectron emphanum,
*Galliformes, Phasianidae), all from Temminck and Laugier de
Chartrouse, 1820-39 (48).*

Plains wanderer (Pedionomus torquatus, Galliformes, Phasianidae), from Gould, 1840-48 (21).

Painted button quail (Turnix varia, Galliformes, Phasianidae), from Temminck and Laugier de Chartrouse, 1820-39 (48).

Hoatzin (Opisthocomus hoatzin, Galliformes, Opisthocomidae), from Cuvier, 1836-49 (9).

Japanese white-necked crane (Grus vipio, Gruiformes, Gruidae), from Temminck and Laugier de Chartrouse, 1820-39 (48).

Hüet.

Grue *à nuque blanche*.

*Above, crowned crane (*Balearica pavonina, *Gruiformes, Gruidae), from Buffon, 1853-57 (5). Below, hooded crane (*Grus monacha, *Gruiformes, Gruidae), from Temminck and Laugier de Chartrouse, 1820-39 (48).*

*Common trumpeter (*Psophia crepitans, *Gruiformes, Psophidae), from Cuvier, 1836-49 (9).*

Grey breasted crake (Laterallus exilis, Gruiformes, Rallidae), from Temminck and Laugier de Chartrouse, 1820-39 (48).

Above, corncrake (Crex crex, Gruiformes, Rallidae), from Donovan, 1794-1819 (13). Right, water rail (Rallus aquaticus, Gruiformes, Rallidae), from Donovan, 1794-1819 (13).

Below, rusty-flanked crake (Laterallus levraudi, Gruiformes, Rallidae), from Zoological Society of London, 1870 (51). Bottom left, spotted crake (Porzana porzana, Gruiformes, Rallidae), from Donovan, 1794-1819 (13).

Banded crake (Rallina eurizonoides, Gruiformes, Rallidae), from Temminck and Laugier de Chartrouse, 1820-39 (48).

Above, giant coot (Fulica gigantea, Gruiformes, Rallidae), from Groenvold and Kirke, 1915-17 (26). Right, common coot (Fulica atra, Gruiformes, Rallidae), from Donovan, 1794-1819 (13).

Right, purple gallinule (Porphyrio porphyrio, Gruiformes, Rallidae), from Buffon, 1853-57 (5).

Above, spot-flanked gallinule (Gallinula melanops, Gruiformes, Rallidae), from Gay, 1844-71 (19). Right, sun-bittern (Eurypyga helias, Gruiformes, Eurypygidae), from Cuvier, 1836-49 (9).

Above, little bustard (Tetrax tetrax, Gruiformes, Otididae), from Buffon, 1853-57 (5).

Above left, lesser florican (Sypheotides indica, Gruiformes, Otididae), from Temminck and Laugier de Chartrouse, 1820-39 (48).Below left, blue bustard (Eupodotis caerulescens, Gruiformes, Otididae), from Temminck and Laugier de Chartrouse, 1820-39 (48).

Red-legged seriema (Cariama cristata, Gruiformes, Cariamidae), from Temminck and Laugier de Chartrouse, 1820-39 (48).

Top right, Australian bustard (Choriotis australis, Gruiformes, Otididae), from Zoological Society of London, 1870 (51). Right, great bustard (Otis tarda, Gruiformes, Otididae), from Loche, 1844-67 (34).

Collecting the unknown:
an explorer, a soldier, and a missionary

Nineteenth-century voyages of exploration to the interior of little-known countries contributed to the discovery of some interesting specimens of fauna and flora and led to a large production of reports with detailed descriptions of the collected scientific materials, often illustrated with refined elegance. A famous person in the Anglo-Saxon ornithological literature is Sir Andrew Smith, one of the first travelers to set out on expeditions for naturalistic explorations inside the territories of southern Africa, at the time still unknown. He discovered many animal species (especially mammals and birds), which he described in detail with marvelous color pictures in a voluminous publication, *Illustrations of the Zoology of South Africa*, the result of his travels effected from 1834 to 1836 (see for instance the martial eagle at page 57). He had already published a few scientific notes in the *South African Quarterly Journal*, also with descriptions of new species of birds captured in South Africa for his ornithological collection; these specimens had been remarkably prepared by the famous French taxidermists the Verreaux brothers, at the time residing in Cape Town. In the course of his last expedition Smith had even brought back about 3500 skins of new and rare South African birds. After his final return to England in 1837, Smith decided to organize an exhibition of his naturalistic collections for the London public in the Egyptian hall in Piccadilly, complete with catalogue on sale at the price of one shilling. Much to Sir Andrew's regret, since he had endured so many difficulties and discovered many new forms of African animals, the exhibition turned out to be a real failure — according to a biographer — and Smith had to sell his animals.

On June 6, 1838, the whole collection was sold at auction in 559 lots in J.C. and S. Stevens's halls, located in King Street in Covent Garden. The specimens that had been used as standards for the description of new species (i.e., the "types") were bought by the British Museum of Natural History and, fortunately for scientists, they are still there. More birds were bought by P.J. Selby and H.E. Strickland and were then included in the collections of the Cambridge University Zoological Museum; additional lots ended up in private English collections, but a large part of this historical and scientific treasure was dispersed and lost among the buyers.

The ornithological collection of Captain Victor Loche, which had been used as a base model to create the marvelous plates of the work *Explorations Scientifiques de l'Algérie pendant 1840-42* were even more ill-fated. Loche, while following the military expeditions in Algeria, had collected local animals, birds and their eggs, reptiles, fish, mollusks, and insects, examples of almost all the fauna known at the time in that French colony. Furthermore, a first catalogue had been compiled for birds and mammals, and an interesting exhibition of all the animals had been organized in Algiers. The collection was then sold in 1860 to several wealthy collectors; the rich Count Turati of Milan bought almost all the birds, which unfortunately were burnt during the last world war, together with many other valuable materials, in the course of a fire that destroyed the City Museum of Natural History in Milan.

As to the part referring to birds in the *Explorations Scientifiques de l'Algérie*, Loche had written the text, enriching it with personal observations or information given him by reliable persons. The ornithological section was accompanied by fifteen marvelous color-printed plates rectified and improved by hand. The authors of the original drawings were Vaillant and Werner; the engravers were Massard, Guyard, Rebuffet, and Clergé Annedouche. The plates representing falconiformes are considered by experts to be "the most beautiful pictures of predatory birds ever made in France."

The picture of the great bustard (page 98) is certainly no less beautiful, and Loche's text cites some interesting characteristics of the biology of this bird, which at the time was already decreasing in number in North Africa: "The great bustard is now only a bird of occasional passage in Algeria, where it was rather diffused sometime ago. A few isolated birds appear there by the end of February or at the beginning of March, when the rigors of winter and heavy snowfalls force them to leave Europe where they usually live. It is a rather massive bird, heavy, wild, suspicious, always on its guard, ready to fly at the slightest sign of danger, and it is almost impossible to come close to it. However, though it is a shy animal, when forced by hunger, it gets near inhabited areas and it was even seen to seek refuge in the farms and fight for food with poultry. So, a landowner at Hussein-Dey was able to capture two bustards in 1852. When the mating time comes, males fight frequently and challenge one another for the possession of females; in the course of these fights the old males, stronger and more vigorous than the young ones, are nearly always the winners, pursuing and driving away the defeated birds until they move away from the females. They hit each other so violently with their wings, that on the defeated males it is often possible to notice large bruises and parts of the wing under-sides completely deprived of feathers, in correspondence with humerus, radius, and elbow."

Another French traveler, the missionary Armand David, is very well known to students of natural sciences for his sensational zoological discoveries and his explorations in China, carried out in the second half of the last century. The discovery (at least as far as naturalists of the Western world were concerned) of the rare Cervidae now bearing his name, the Father David's deer (*Elaphurus davidianus*), must be ascribed to him. In fact, a few specimens of this animal were confined exclusively inside the imperial park of Peking, and Father David succeeded, after many difficulties, in bribing an imperial guardian in order to obtain from him a few hides that he wanted to send to the Paris museum. In 1869 Father David saw for the first time, as he was having tea in the house of a Chinese landowner, the black and white hide of another animal, entirely unknown to him: it was a trophy of the very rare, and later very famous, giant panda, *Ailuropoda melanoleuca*.

Father David's scientific observations concerning ornithology are collected in *Les Oiseaux de la Chine*, published in 1877 in collaboration with Emile Oustalet of the Musée d'Histoire Naturelle of Paris. During his adventurous excursions across a large area of western and central China from 1867 to 1874, David discovered many new or little-known bird species, among them pheasants and several passeriformes. These new specimens were sent as they were discovered to the Paris museum, where his colleagues Oustalet and Verreaux described them scientifically.

In the journal of his exploration published when he returned to France, Father David often remembers the circumstances of his ornithological discoveries. In connection with the *Ithaginis sinensis* (*Ithaginis cruentus sinensis*, page 85) he writes: "Inkiapo, sixth December 1872. Tonight my hunter Ouang has come back from the high mountains of Laoling, which he found covered by a thick sheet of snow. He accomplished his excursion very quickly. But I am very pleased with him, because he killed and brought back himself a pair of pheasants of a new species..." And he continues: "It is exactly at two days' march from here, south-southwest of Inkiapo, that Ouang met the *Ithaginis* pheasants in the middle of wild bamboos and rhododendrons..." And on December 1 of the same year: "Today, has been dedicated to preparing twelve *Ithaginis sinensis*..."

Woodcocks, plovers, terns, gulls, doves, and parrots

Dodo.

The birds in this chapter include three distinct orders, Charadriiformes, Columbiformes, and Psittaciformes, all with more or less the same number of species. In spite of this apparently uniform number, the order of Charadriiformes is by far the most complicated order, and in fact it is divided into three sub-orders and eighteen families that include species with very different features and habits: limicoline birds, which is to say those living on shorelines, such as curlews, piro-piro, and tattlers; web-footed birds, such as gulls, elegant gliders, and divers such as terns, and sea birds with features and habits resembling those of penguins, such as auks. After much uncertainty, modern DNA-comparing methods have confirmed the common origin of the whole group and the rather close relationship of species distinguished by sometimes very different specific qualities.

Each of the remaining two orders is very uniform, so that even people who are not interested in ornithology can generally recognize with no difficulty a pigeon or a parrot. However, the Columbiformes include not only Columbidae but also Pteroclidae, which at first sight look more like partridges than pigeons or turtle-doves.

Above, northern jacana (Jacana spinosa, Charadriiformes, Jacanidae), from Cory, 1885 (8). Right, pheasant-tailed jacana (Hydrophasianus chirurgus, Charadriiformes, Jacanidae), from Gould, 1850-83 (23).

Below left, comb-crested jacana (Irediparra gallinacea, Charadriiformes, Jacanidae), from Temminck and Laugier de Chartrouse, 1820-39 (48). Below right, South American painted snipe (Nycticryphes semicollaris, Charadriiformes, Rostratulidae), from Cuvier, 1836-49 (9).

Below, oystercatcher (Haematopus ostralegus, Charadriiformes, Haematopodidae), from Catesby, 1754 (6)

M. Catesby ad viv. del.

I.M. Seligmann sc. et excud.

C.P.S. Cas. Majest.

Haemotapus Will. p. 297 Bellon. Lib. p. 209.

No. 70 W. Theil.

Le Preneur d'Huiſtres

*Below left, Javanese wattled lapwing (*Vanellus macropterus, *Charadriiformes, Charadriidae), from Temminck and Laugier de Chartrouse, 1820-39 (48). Below right, white-crowned wattled plover (*Vanellus albiceps, *Charadriiformes, Charadriidae), from Temminck and Laugier de Chartrouse, 1820-39 (48).*

*Below left, spur-winged plover (*Vanellus spinosus, *Charadriiformes, Charadriidae), from Cuvier, 1836-49 (9). Below right, Kittlitz's sand plover (*Charadrius pecuarius, *Charadriiformes, Charadriidae), from Temminck and Laugier de Chartrouse, 1820-39 (48).*

Right, lapwing (Vanellus vanellus, Charadriiformes, Charadriidae), from Buffon, 1853-57 (5). Center, golden plover (Pluvialis apricaria, Charadriiformes, Charadriidae), from Cuvier, 1836-49 (9). Below, grey plover (Pluvialis squatarola, Charadriiformes, Charadriidae), from Albin, 1731-38 (1).

Left, purple sandpiper (Calidris maritima, Charadriiformes, Scolopacidae), from Gaimard, 1838-52 (18). Below left, bar-tailed godwit (Limosa lapponica, Charadriiformes, Scolopacidae), from Donovan, 1794-1819 (13). Below right, turnstone (Arenaria interpres, Charadriiformes, Scolopacidae), from Cuvier, 1836-49 (9).

Redshank (Tringa totanus,
Charadriiformes, Scolopacidae),
from Donovan, 1794-1819 (13).

Above, culew (Numenius
arquata, Charadriiformes,
Scolopacidae), from Buffon,
1853-57 (5). Below right, giant
snipe (Gallinago undulata,
Charadriiformes, Scolopacidae),
from Temminck and Laugier de
Chartrouse, 1820-39 (48).

Whimbrel (Numenius phaeopus, Charadriiformes,
Scolopacidae), from Donovan, 1794-1819 (13).

Above left, turnstone (Arenaria interpres, Charadriiformes, Scolopacidae). Above right, black-winged stilt (Himantopus himantopus, Charadriiformes, Recurvirostridae). Below, avocet (Recurvirostra avosetta, Charadriiformes, Recurvirostridae), all from Buffon, 1853-57 (5).

Fournier sc.

Pardinel sc.

*Ibis bill (*Ibidorhyncha struthersii, *Charadriiformes, Recurvirostridae), from David, 1877 (10).*

Grey phalarope (Phalaropus fulicarius, Charadriiformes, Phalaropodidae), from Cuvier, 1836-49 (9).

*Left, Wilson's phalarope (*Phalaropus tricolor, *Charadriiformes, Phalaropodidae), from Temminck and Laugier de Chartrouse, 1820-39 (48). Right, crab plover (*Dromas ardeola, *Charadriiformes, Dromadidae), from Temminck and Laugier de Chartrouse, 1820-39 (48).*

*Below left and bottom right, grey-breasted seedsnipe (*Thinocorus orbignyanus, *Charadriiformes, Tinocoridae), from Lesson, 1830-32 (30). Below right, Australian pratincole (*Stiltia isabella, *Charadriiformes, Glareolidae), from Cuvier, 1836-49 (9).*

*Left, bronze-winged courser (*Rhinoptilus chalcopterus, *Charadriiformes, Glareolidae), from Temminck and Laugier de Chartrouse, 1820-39 (48).*

Below right, Egyptian plovers (Pluvianus aegyptius, Charadriiformes, Glareolidae), from Gould, 1850-83 (23).

Above left, great Australian stone plover (Esacus magnirostris, Charadriiformes, Burinidae), from Temminck and Laugier de Chartrouse, 1820-39 (48).

Above and right, snowy sheathbill (Chionis alba, Charadriiformes, Chionididae), from Cuvier, 1836-49 (9).

Iceland gull (Larus glaucoides, Charadriiformes, Laridae), from Gaimard, 1838-52 (18).

White-eyed gull (Larus leucophtalmus, Charadriiformes, Laridae), from Temminck and Laugier de Chartrouse, 1820-39 (48).

Above left, silver gull (Cereopsis novaehollandiae, Anseriformes, Anatidae), from Temminck and Laugier de Chartrouse, 1820-39 (48). Above right, Pacific gull (Gabianus pacificus, Charadriiformes, Laridae), from Temminck and Laugier de Chartrouse, 1820-39 (48).

Below right, little tern (Thalasseus sandvicensis, Charadriiformes, Laridae), from Donovan, 1794-1819 (13). Below, black-bellied tern (Sterna melanogaster, Charadriiformes, Laridae), from Gould, 1850-53 (23).

Above, black skimmer (Rynchops niger, Charadriiformes, Rynchopidae), from D'Orbigny, 1837 (15). Right, little tern (Sterna albifrons, Charadriiformes, Laridae), from Donovan, 1794-1819 (13).

Atlantic puffin (Fratercula arctica, Charadriiformes, Alcidae), from Cuvier, 1836-49 (9).

Right and above right, razorbill (Alca torda, Charadriiformes, Alcidae), from Cuvier, 1836-49 (9).

Above left, crested auklet (Aethia cristatella, Charadriiformes, Alcidae), from Temminck and Laugier de Chartrouse, 1820-39 (48). Above right, crested murrelet (Synthlihoramphus wumizusume, Charadriiformes, Alcidae), from Temminck and Laugier de Chartrouse, 1820-39 (48). Left, black guillemot (Cepphus grylle, Charadriiformes, Alcidae), from Gaimard, 1838-52 (18).

Yellow-throated sandgrouse (Pterocles gutturalis, Columbiformes, Pteroclidae), from Temminck and Laugier de Chartrouse, 1820-39 (48).

Below, Pallas' sandgrouse (Syrrhaptes paradoxus, Columbiformes, Pteroclidae), from Temminck and Laugier de Chartrouse, 1820-39 (48). Bottom, left and right, Lichtenstein's sandgrouse (Pterocles lichtensteinii, Columbiformes, Pteroclidae), from Temminck and Laugier de Chartrouse, 1820-39 (48).

117

Eastern turtle dove (Streptopelia orientalis, Columbiformes, Columbidae), from Temminck and Laugier de Chartrouse, 1820-39 (48).

Magnificent fruit dove (Ptilinopus magnificus, Columbiformes, Columbidae), from Temminck and Laugier de Chartrouse, 1820-39 (48).

Above left, crimson-capped fruit dove (Ptilinopus pulchellus, Columbiformes, Columbidae), from Temminck and Laugier de Chartrouse, 1820-39 (48). Above right, dodo (Raphus cucullatus, Columbiformes, Rafidae), from Pouchet, 1841 (42).

*Black-collared fruit pigeon
(*Ducula mullerii,
*Columbiformes,
Columbidae), from
Temminck and Laugier de
Chartrouse, 1820-39 (48).*

*Pink-spotted fruit dove
(*Ptilinopus perlatus,
*Columbiformes, Columbidae),
from Temminck and Laugier de
Chartrouse, 1820-39 (48).*

*Celebes pied imperial pigeon
(*Ducula luctuosa,
*Columbiformes,
Columbidae), from
Temminck and Laugier de
Chartrouse, 1820-39 (48).*

*Partridge bronzewing (*Petrophassa
scripta, *Columbiformes, Columbidae),
from Temminck and Laugier de
Chartrouse, 1820-39 (48).*

*Below left, crested pigeon (Ocyphaps lophotes, Columbiformes, Columbidae), from Temminck and Laugier de Chartrouse, 1820-39 (48). Below right, white-bellied wedge-tailed green pigeon (*Treron sieboldii, *Columbiformes, Columbidae), from Temminck and Laugier de Chartrouse, 1820-39 (48). Below, turtle dove (*Streptopelia turtur, *Columbiformes, Columbidae), from Buffon, 1853-57 (5).*

*Major Mitchell's cockatoo
(Cacatua leadbeateri,
Psittaciformes, Psittacidae), from
Selby, 1836 (44).*

*Palm cockatoo (Probosciger
aterrimus, Psittaciformes,
Psittacidae), from Cuvier, 1836-49
(9).*

*Goffin's cockatoo (Cacatua
goffini, Psittaciformes, Psittacidae),
from Temminck and Laugier de
Chartrouse, 1820-39 (48).*

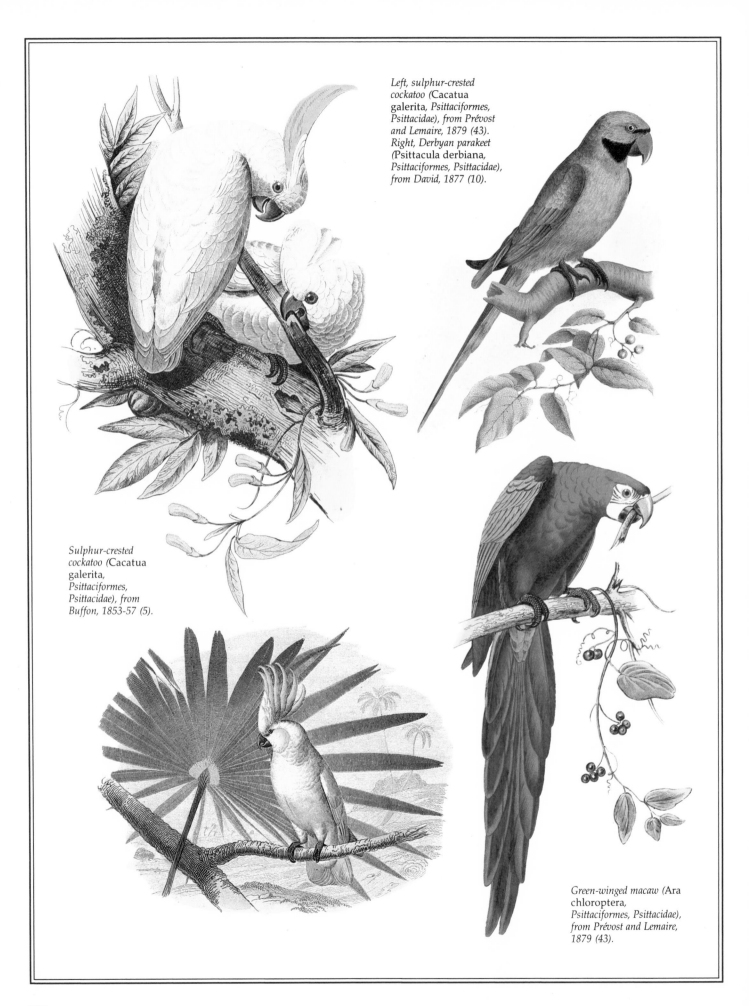

Left, sulphur-crested
cockatoo (Cacatua
galerita, *Psittaciformes,
Psittacidae), from Prévost
and Lemaire, 1879 (43).
Right, Derbyan parakeet
(Psittacula derbiana,
Psittaciformes, Psittacidae),
from David, 1877 (10).*

*Sulphur-crested
cockatoo (Cacatua
galerita,
Psittaciformes,
Psittacidae), from
Buffon, 1853-57 (5).*

*Green-winged macaw (Ara
chloroptera,
Psittaciformes, Psittacidae),
from Prévost and Lemaire,
1879 (43).*

Yellow-streaked lory
(Chalcopsitta sintillata,
*Psittaciformes, Psittacidae),
from Temminck and Laugier de
Chartrouse, 1820-39 (48).*

Red-flanked lorikeet
(Charmosyna placentis,
*Psittaciformes, Psittacidae),
from Temminck and Laugier de
Chartrouse, 1820-39 (48).*

Iris lorikeet (Trichoglossus
iris, *Psittaciformes, Psittacidae),
from Temminck and Laugier de
Chartrouse, 1820-39 (48).*

Below, golden-mantled racket-tailed parrot (Prioniturus platurus, *Psittaciformes, Psittacidae), from Temminck and Laugier de Chartrouse, 1820-39 (48).*

Red-spectacled Amazon (Amazona preteri, *Psittaciformes, Psittacidae), from Temminck and Laugier de Chartrouse, 1820-39 (48).*

Above, blue-throated conure (Pyrrhura cruentata, *Psittaciformes, Psittacidae). Right, scarlet-shouldered parrot* (Touit huetii, *Psittaciformes, Psittacidae), both from Temminck and Laugier de Chartrouse, 1820-39 (48).*

*Above, Northern rosella (*Platycercus venustus, *Psittaciformes, Psittacidae), from Donovan, 1834 (14). Right, Eastern rosella (*Platycercus eximius, *Psittaciformes, Psittacidae), from Levaillant, 1801-05 (32).*

125

Below left, green rosella (Platycercus caledonicus, Psittaciformes, Psittacidae), from Levaillant, 1801-05 (32). Below right, black-winged parrot (Hapalopsittaca melanotis, Psittaciformes, Psittacidae), from Donovan, 1834 (14).

Left, golden-winged parakeet (Brotogeris chrysopteus, Psittaciformes, Psittacidae), from Donovan, 1834 (14). Right, cardinal lory (Chalcopsitta cardinalis, Psittaciformes, Psittacidae), from Zoological Society of London, 1870 (51).

The difficulties of ornithological painting: adding a touch of naturalness to stuffed birds

Columbidae and Psittacidae are two groups of birds with very uniform general features but vividly contrasting and brightly colored feathers. No wonder, then, that many 18th- and 19th-century writers of ornithological books have chosen them often as subjects for their large monographs – enriched by accurately engraved pictures with the finishing touch of a light stroke of brush in tempera. In his very famous *Histoire Naturelle*, Buffon described the macaw in his typical style: "Among all parrots, the macaw is the largest and most magnificently adorned. Red, gold, and blue shine on its feathers. It has firm eyes, a serious countenance, slow movements, and even an unpleasantly disdainful expression, as if it guessed its value and was well aware of its beauty."

In the plates of their *Nouveau recueil de planches coloriées*, Temminck and Laugier lay stress on the new pigeon and parrot species (such as, for instance, the pink-spotted fruit dove on page 119 and the red-spectacled Amazon on page 124) brought back from voyages to the southern hemisphere and assembled in the large collections of the Paris, Berlin, Amsterdam, Vienna, and Leiden museums. They are shown in many pictures, and great accuracy is devoted to the colors of their feathers. Though these are stuffed and reconstructed models, the painters of this book work true "miracles" to make them look as alive and real as possible, especially the pigeons, and all are provided with very soft and delicate-looking feathers. The artists knew very well their aim in this naturalistic representation and the necessary limits required by their authors. Temminck, in fact, had underlined this in the introductory text: "No human language can clearly describe so many undefined nuances, represent all the spots, lines, stripes, dots, composing the colors of the feathers, nor could it make us understand the more or less brilliant, more or less sweet, more or less bizarre

general effect resulting from the combination or opposition of all these hues. The help of a painter is absolutely necessary. The authors offer the readers a collection of colored plates having as main subject birds not represented in Buffon's illuminated tables.

"Natural history illustrations must be carried out according to particular rules. So the artist must avoid unnatural postures, angulations that might give a wrong idea of the true shape of each single part. He must distribute light evenly and show in all parts the essential colors with no alterations caused by bright reflections or too deep shadows."

Temminck's directions to the artist had previously been applied by a collaborator of his, Pauline de Courcelles, a pupil of the famous painter Jacques Barraband, in another text written by Temminck to illustrate pigeons: *Histoire Naturelle Générale des Pigeons*, published in 1808. Mademoiselle de Courcelles, married later to the Dutch painter of floral subjects Joseph August Knip, had developed a quite new technique to represent the slightly powdery pastel hues of pigeons' feathers by using an opaque kind of tempera. She contacted Temminck, and they decided together to issue a monograph about Columbidae, with a text written, as usual, by Temminck, and plates drawn and colored by Madame Knip de Courcelles.

The first part, published in 1808, was dedicated to Louis Napoleon Bonaparte, at the time king of Holland, and it was at once a great public success in spite of its remarkable price. The identification of several new species by Temminck in the natural history museums of almost all Europe, together with their lifelike pictures, began to win renown for the young Dutch ornithologist. Later, on returning from the Amsterdam museums where he had studied and prepared new subjects to be published in the next issues of *Pigeons*, Temminck had a bitter surprise: taking advantage of her co-author's absence, Madame Knip had in the meantime published the remaining numbers of the work (from the 9th to the 15th number) using only her name on the title page. Very likely, Pauline meant to impress the new French Empress, Mary Louise of Austria, to whom she had dedicated her work and from whom she had received the much valued appointment of "Her Majesty's first Natural History painter." As a consequence, Temminck and Madame Knip broke their collaboration, and the great monograph remained unfinished.

Shortly after, the glory of the Napoleonic Empire vanished and with it went the costly fashion of large picture monographs. Only after many years did Madame Knip succeed in publishing about seventy more plates of Columbidae, with the scientific help of an assistant naturalist of the Paris museum, Florent Prévost. According to some biographers, she had probably become reconciled with Coenraad Temminck at the time because her former co-author entrusted her with the reproductions of some new species of pigeons just brought back by the Dutch East India Company.

One of the most outstanding 19th-century ornithological books is the *Histoire Naturelle des Perroquets* by a Frenchman, François Levaillant, published in Paris from 1801 to 1805 in two large in-folio volumes (see for example the Eastern rosella and the green rosella at pages 125 and 126). This work has nowadays become very rare, and complete editions reach astronomic prices. Unfortunately, because of the beauty of its plates and the perfection of their execution, this work has been inevitably "broken" several times and sold on the antiquarian market as separate pictures to be put in frames. The 145 plates are by the French painter Jacques Barraband, an artist who specialized in floral and naturalistic decorations. Also, in this case, the artist used as models some specimens of "stuffed" parrots, and his draw-

ings, however perfect, sometimes betray the "not alive" appearance of the reproduced subjects. But the lorikeets and Amazons are really splendid and often attain almost perfection.

Barraband engaged also in the profitable career of decorator artist for the Sèvres porcelain and other French arts manufacturers, such as tapestry, for which a particular skill was required for the elegant representation of flower festoons, fruit, and birds in naturalistic designs.

François Levaillant, the author of this grand monograph about Psittaciformes, was a man characterized by an indomitably enterprising spirit: as a young man he had traveled often, exploring the interior of southern Africa, and in a more mature age he had devoted himself to scientific collecting and to the economically profitable writing of autobiographic books about his travels and costly picture monographs about various tropical avifaunas. The Viscount von Hoffmannsegg, who visited him in Paris in 1797, said of him: "Levaillant is a man of about forty, of a medium height with handsome regular features and intelligent piercing eyes; his genius is easily recognizable, but he is certainly not formal. It is quite possible that he often exaggerates his tales, 'embellishing' what he has seen in the course of his travels, but certainly not so much as we are led to believe. I had never been able to understand how he succeeded in preparing taxidermically so many birds in one day, as he maintained; so I asked him. He assured me that it wouldn't take him longer than three minutes to prepare a small bird for the collection, which I thought exaggerated. So he asked immediately for a small bird and started preparing it completely right before us; in less than three minutes' time he had finished! He told me later that sometimes it happened to him to kill about thirty or more birds in one day, and he always succeeded in preparing them all on the same day."

Cuckoos, nocturnal predatory birds, hummingbirds, hoopoes, and woodpeckers

The birds described in this chapter belong to eight different
orders with a total of thirty families. Four of these orders are
rather homogeneous: no one would hesitate to recognize a
nocturnal bird of prey (Strigiformes), a goatsucker
(Caprimulgiformes), an African mouse-bird (Coliiformes), or a
trogon (Trogoniformes). The other four orders are instead rather
diverse: Cuculiformes include, beside the well-known cuckoos,
also the marvelous touraco; Apodiformes include such different
birds as swifts and hummingbirds; Coraciiformes and
Piciformes constitute two miscellanies of very different families
with few anatomical features in common.

   Among the different groups considered here, the most
numerous are represented by hummingbirds and woodpeckers;
they are followed by Strigidae, cuckoos, kingfishers, swifts, and
the goatsuckers. On the other side, there are some orders, such as
the Coliiformes, that consist of six species in all and some
families, such as the arboreal swift family, that have only four
species, or the Upupidae or the Leptosomatidae, which currently
consist of one single species each.

Hartlaub's turaco (Tauraco hartlaubi, Cuculiformes, Musophagidae), from Smith, 1838-49 (45).

Right, Knysna turaco (Tauraco corythaix, Cuculiformes, Musophagidae), from Temminck and Laugier de Chartrouse, 1820-39 (48). Far right, great blue turacos (Corythaeola cristata, Cuculiformes, Musophagidae), from Temminck and Laugier de Chartrouse, 1820-39 (48).

Giant Madagascar coucal
(*Coua gigas*,
Cuculiformes, Cuculidae),
*from Temminck and
Laugier de Chartrouse,
1820-39 (48).*

Above left, great spotted cuckoo (Clamator glandarius,
Cuculiformes, Cuculidae). *Above right,*
channel-billed cuckoo (Scythrops novaehollandiae,
Cuculiformes, Cuculidae), *both from Temminck
and Laugier de Chartrouse, 1820-39 (48).*

Top, African emerald cuckoo (Chrysococcyx cupreus, Cuculiformes, Cuculidae), from Prévost and Lemaire, 1879 (43). Center, running coucal (Coua cursor, Cuculiformes, Cuculidae), from Temminck and Laugier de Chartrouse, 1820-39 (48). Bottom, koel (Eudynamys scolopacea, Cuculiformes, Cuculidae), from Leach, 1814-17 (27).

Left, rufous-vented ground cuckoo
(Neomorphus geoffroyi, Cuculiformes,
Cuculidae), from Temminck and Laugier de
Chartrouse, 1820-39 (48). Right, didric cuckoo
(Chrysococcyx caprius, Cuculiformes,
Cuculidae), from Prévost and Lemaire, 1879
(43).

Celebes malcoha (Ramphococcix
calyorhynchus, Cuculiformes,
Cuculidae), from Temminck and
Laugier de Chartrouse, 1820-39
(48).

Greater coucal (Centropus
menbeki, Cuculiformes,
Cuculidae), from Lesson, 1826-
30 (28).

Left, rusty barred owl
(Strix hylophila,
Strigiformes, Strigidae),
from Temminck and
Laugier de Chartrouse,
1820-39 (48). Right, barred
owlet (Glaucidium
capense, Strigiformes,
Strigidae), from Smith,
1838-49 (45).

Hawk owl (Surnia ulula,
Strigiformes, Strigidae),
from Edwards, 1743-51
(17).

Barn owl (Tyto alba, Strigiformes, Tytonidae), from Smith, 1838-49 (45).

Little owl (Athene noctua, Strigiformes, Strigidae), from Donovan, 1794-1819 (13).

Tawny owl (Strix aluco, Strigiformes, Strigidae), from Donovan, 1794-1819 (13).

Above right, African wood owl (Ciccaba woodfordii, Strigiformes, Strigidae), from Smith, 1838-49 (45). Below right, bay owl (Phodilus badius, Strigiformes, Tytonidae), from Temminck and Laugier de Chartrouse, 1820-39 (48).

Below left, cape eagle owl (Bubo capensis, Strigiformes, Strigidae), from Smith, 1838-49 (45). Below right, collared scops owl (Otus bakkamoena, Strigiformes, Strigidae), from Pennant, 1790 (40).

Barn owl (Tyto alba, Strigiformes, Tytonidae), from Donovan, 1794-1819 (13).

White-faced scops owl (Otus leucotis, Strigiformes, Strigidae), from Temminck and Laugier de Chartrouse, 1820-39 (48).

African scops owl (Otus senegalensis, Strigiformes, Strigidae), from Smith, 1838-49 (45).

Verreaux's eagle owl (Bubo lacteus, Strigiformes, Strigidae), from Temminck and Laugier de Chartrouse, 1820-39 (48).

Above left, eagle owl (Bubo bubo, Strigiformes, Strigidae), from David, 1877 (10). Above right, spotted eagle owl (Bubo africanus, Strigiformes, Strigidae), from Temminck and Laugier de Chartrouse, 1820-39 (48).

*Above, jungle nightjar (*Caprimulgus indicus, *Caprimulgiformes, Caprimulgidae), from Gray, 1830-34 (25). Above right and bottom right, scissor-tailed nightjar (*Hydropsalis brasiliana, *Caprimulgiformes, Caprimulgidae), from Temminck and Laugier de Chartrouse, 1820-39 (48). Center right, Indian nightjar (*Caprimulgus asiaticus, *Caprimulgiformes, Caprimulgidae), from Gray, 1830-34 (25).*

Left, Javan frogmouth (Batrachostomus javensis, *Caprimulgiformes, Padargidae*), from Temminck and Laugier de Chartrouse, 1820-39 (48). Right, Wallace's owlet-nightjar (Aegotheles wallacii, *Caprimulgiformes, Aegothelidae*), from Gould, 1875-88 (24).

Above left, Papuan frogmouth (Podargus papuensis, *Caprimulgiformes, Podargidae*), from Comte, 1830 (7). Above right, golden nightjar (Caprimulgus eximius, *Caprimulgiformes, Caprimulgidae*), from Temminck and Laugier de Chartrouse, 1820-39 (48).

*White-throated spinetail swift (*Hirundapus caudacuta, *Apodiformes, Apodidae), from Dubois, 1905 (16).*

*Above, white-rumped swiftlet (*Collocalia spodiopygia, *Apodiformes, Apodidae), from Gould, 1875-88 (24). Right, Cassin's spinetailed swift (*Neafrapus cassini, *Apodiformes, Apodidae), from Zoological Society of London, 1870 (51).*

*Asian palm swift (*Cypsiurus batasiensis, *Apodiformes, Apodidae), from Gray, 1830-34 (25).*

*Lesser tree swift (*Hemiprocne comata, *Apodiformes, Hemiprocnidae), from Temminck and Laugier de Chartrouse, 1820-39 (48).*

*Indian crested tree swift (*Hemiprocne coronata, *Apodiformes, Hemiprocnidae), from Temminck and Laugier de Chartrouse, 1820-39 (48).*

Brazilian ruby (Clytolaema rubricauda, *Apodiformes, Trochilidae), from Gould, 1849-61 (22).*

Below and right, two kinds
of Andean hillstar
(Oreotrochilus estella,
Apodiformes, Trochilidae),
from Gould, 1849-61 (22).

Merida sunangel
(Heliangelus spencei,
Apodiformes, Trochilidae),
from Gould, 1849-61 (22).

Saw-billed hermit
(Ramphodon naevius,
Apodiformes, Trochilidae),
from Gould, 1849-61 (22).

Left, crimson topaz (Topaza pella, *Apodiformes, Trochilidae), from Donovan, 1834 (14). Below, tufted coquette* (Lophornis ornata, *Apodiformes, Trochilidae), from Donovan, 1834 (14).*

Above, blue-headed sapphire (Hylocharis grayi, *Apodiformes, Trochilidae), from Mulsant, 1874-77 (39), and (right) from Lesson, 1829-30 (29).*

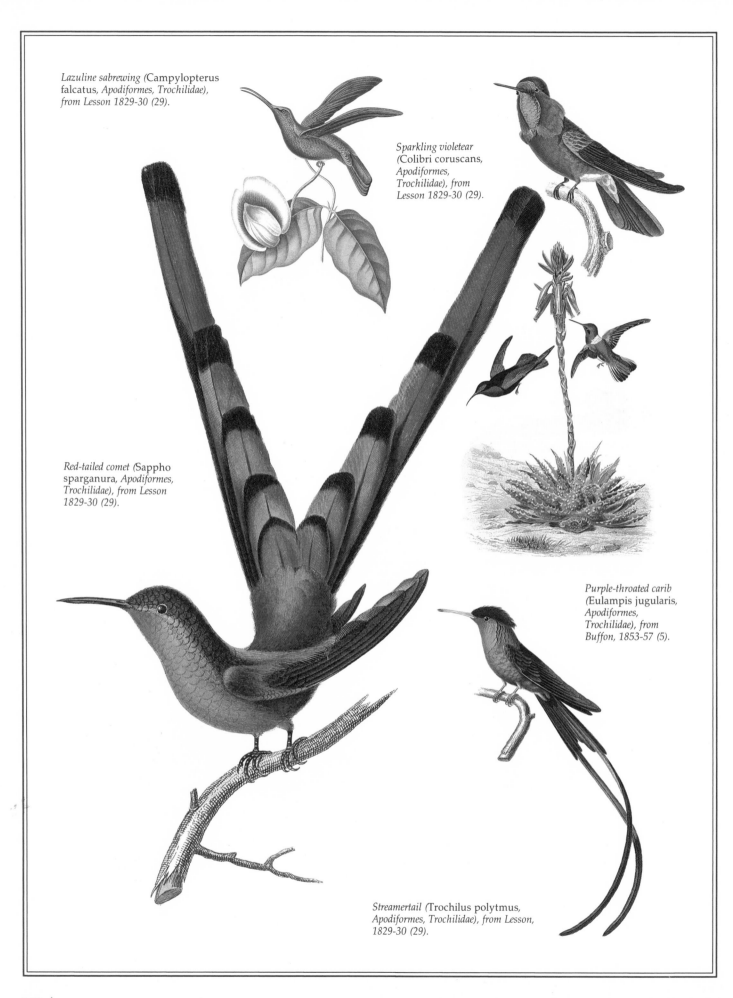

Lazuline sabrewing (Campylopterus falcatus, *Apodiformes, Trochilidae*), from Lesson 1829-30 (29).

Sparkling violetear (Colibri coruscans, *Apodiformes, Trochilidae*), from Lesson 1829-30 (29).

Red-tailed comet (Sappho sparganura, *Apodiformes, Trochilidae*), from Lesson 1829-30 (29).

Purple-throated carib (Eulampis jugularis, *Apodiformes, Trochilidae*), from Buffon, 1853-57 (5).

Streamertail (Trochilus polytmus, *Apodiformes, Trochilidae*), from Lesson, 1829-30 (29).

146

*Horned sungem
(Heliactin cornuta,
Apodiformes,
Trochilidae), from
Lesson, 1829-30 (29).*

*Red-backed mousebird
(Colius castanotus,
Coliiformes, Coliidae),
from Cuvier, 1836-49
(9).*

*Right, black-bellied
thorntail (Popelairia
langsdorffi,
Apodiformes,
Trochilidae), from
Prévost and Lemaire,
1879 (43). Below, giant
hummingbird
(Patagona gigas,
Apodiformes,
Trochilidae), from
Lesson, 1829-30 (29).*

*Resplendent quetzal (Pharomachrus mocinno,
Trogoniformes, Trogonidae), from D'Orbigny, 1837 (15).*

Above left, white-tipped quetzal (Pharomachrus fulgidus, Trogoniformes, Trogonidae), from Temminck and Laugier de Chartrouse, 1820-39 (48). Above, right, Narina's trogon (Apaloderma narina, Trogoniformes, Trogonidae), from Gould, 1838 (20). Below, Hispaniolan trogon (Temnotrogon roseigaster, Trogoniformes, Trogonidae), from Cory, 1885 (8).

Left, Diard's trogon (Harpactes diardii, Trogoniformes, Trogonidae). Center, scarlet-rumped trogon (Harpactes duvaucelii, Trogoniformes, Trogonidae). Right, Malabar trogon (Harpactes fasciatus, Trogoniformes, Trogonidae), all from Temminck and Laugier de Chartrouse, 1820-39 (48).

Top, greater pied kingfisher (Ceryle lugubris, Coraciiformes, Alcedinidae), from Temminck and Laugier de Chartrouse, 1820-39 (48). Above, dwarf kingfisher (Ceyx lepidus, Coraciiformes, Alcedinidae), from Temminck and Laugier de Chartrouse, 1820-39 (48). Left, Celebes blue-eared kingfisher (Cittura cyanotis, Coraciiformes, Alcedinidae), from Zoological Society of London, 1870 (51).

Top left, woodland kingfisher (Halcyon senegalensis, Coraciiformes, Alcedinidae), from Smith, 1838-49 (45). Left, common kingfisher (Alcedo atthis, Coraciiformes, Alcedinidae), from Donovan, 1794-1819 (13). Above, chestnut-collared kingfisher (Halcyon concreta, Coraciiformes, Alcedinidae), from Temminck and Laugier de Chartrouse, 1820-39 (48).

Above, banded kingfisher (Lacedo pulchella, Coraciiformes, Alcedinidae), from Temminck and Laugier de Chartrouse, 1820-39 (48). Right, black-capped kingfisher (Halcyon pileata, Coraciiformes, Alcedinidae), from Lesson, 1830-32 (30). Below, black-bellied kingfisher (Pelargopsis melanorhyncha, Coraciiformes, Alcedinidae), from Temminck and Laugier de Chartrouse, 1820-39 (48).

Top left, European bee-eater (Merops apiaster, Coraciiformes, Meropidae), from Cuvier, 1836-49 (9). Top right, Jamaican tody (Todus todus, Coraciiformes, Todidae), from Cuvier, 1836-49 (9).

Above left, blue-crowned motmot (Momotus momota, Coraciiformes, Momotidae), from Cuvier, 1836-49 (9). Above right, white-fronted bee-eater (Merops bullockoides, Coraciiformes, Meropidae), from Smith, 1838-49 (45).

Below left, common roller (Coracias garrulus, Coraciiformes, Coraciidae), from Cuvier, 1836-49 (9). Below right, red-bearded bee-eater (Nyctiornis amicta, Coraciiformes, Meropidae), from Temminck and Laugier de Chartrouse, 1820-39 (48).

Above left, blue-bellied roller (Coracias cyanogaster, Coraciiformes, Coraciidae), from Prévost and Lemaire, 1879 (43). Above right, Indian roller (Coracias benghalensis, Coraciiformes, Coraciidae), from Gould, 1850-53 (23).

Top right, rufous hornbill (Buceros hydrocorax, Coraciiformes, Bucerotidae), from Temminck and Laugier de Chartrouse, 1820-39 (48). Right, green wood hoopoe (Phoeniculus purpureus, Coraciiformes, Phoeniculidae), from D'Orbigny, 1837 (15). Below, hoopoe (Upupa epops, Coraciiformes, Upupidae), from D'Orbigny, 1837 (15).

Left, rhinoceros hornbill (Buceros rhinoceros, Coraciiformes, Bucerotidae), from Temminck and Laugier de Chartrouse, 1820-39 (48). Below, black-casqued hornbill (Ceratogymma atrata, Coraciiformes, Bucerotidae), from Temminck and Laugier de Chartrouse, 1820-39 (48).

Above, Celebes hornbill (Aceros cassidix, Coraciiformes, Bucerotidae), from Temminck and Laugier de Chartrouse, 1820-39 (48). Below, Temminck's hornbill (Penelopides exaratus, Coraciiformes, Bucerotidae), from Temminck and Laugier de Chartrouse, 1820-39 (48).

Top left, long-crested hornbill
(Berenicornis comatus, *Coraciiformes,*
Bucerotidae), from Mueller, 1839-44 (38).
Left, yellow-billed jacamar (Galbula
albirostris, *Piciformes, Galbulidae),* from
Donovan, 1834 (14). Above, wrinkled
hornbill (Aceros corrugatus,
Coraciiformes, Bucerotidae), from
Temminck and Laugier de Chartrouse,
1820-39 (48).

Left, green-tailed jacammar (Galbula galbula) and paradise jacammar (Galbula dea, Piciformes, Galbulidae), from Prévost and Lemaire, 1879 (43).

Left, pale-headed jacammar (Brachygalba goeringi, Piciformes, Galbulidae), from Zoological Society of London, 1870 (51). Above, white-eared jacammar (Galbalcyrhynchus leucotis, Piciformes, Galbulidae), from Dubois, 1905 (16).

Left, white-necked puffbird (Notharchus macrorhynchus) and collared puffbird (Bucco capensis, Piciformes, Bucconidae), from Prévost and Lemaire, 1879 (43). Below, fire-tufted barbet (Psilopogon pyrolophus, Piciformes, Capitonidae), from Temminck and Laugier de Chartrouse, 1820-39 (48). Bottom right, black-collared barbet (Lybius torquatus, Piciformes, Capitonidae), from Temminck and Laugier de Chartrouse, 1820-39 (48).

Above, white-necked puffbird (Notharcus macrorhynchos) and collared puffbird (Bucco capensis, Piciformes, Bucconidae), from Buffon, 1853-57 (5)

*Below left, yellow-crowned barbet (*Megalaima henricii, *Piciformes, Capitonidae), from Temminck and Laugier de Chartrouse, 1820-39 (48). Left, gold-whiskered barbet (*Megalaima chrysopogon, *Piciformes, Capitonidae), from Temminck and Laugier de Chartrouse, 1820-39 (48). Bottom, lemon-throated barbet (*Eubucco richardsoni, *Piciformes, Capitonidae), from Buffon, 1853-57 (5).*

Top left, lesser honeyguide (Indicator minor, Piciformes, Indicatoridae), from Temminck and Laugier de Chartrouse, 1820-39 (48). Top right, black-throated honeyguide (Indicator indicator, Piciformes, Indicatoridae), from Temminck and Laugier de Chartrouse, 1820-39 (48). Above left, channel-billed toucan (Ramphastos vitellinus, Piciformes, Ramphastidae), from D'Orbigny, 1837 (15).

Above left, Malay honeyguide (Indicator archipelagus, Piciformes, Indicatoridae), from Temminck and Laugier de Chartrouse, 1820-39 (48). Above, groove-billed toucanet (Aulacorhynchus sulcatus, Piciformes, Ramphastidae), from Temminck and Laugier de Chartrouse, 1820-39 (48).

Green aracari (Pteroglossus viridis, Piciformes, Ramphastidae), from Donovan, 1834 (14).

Above, checker-throated woodpecker (Picus mentalis, Piciformes, Picidae), from Temminck and Laugier de Chartrouse, 1820-39 (48). Right, wryneck (Jinx torquilla, Piciformes, Picidae), from Donovan, 1794-1819 (13).

Banded red woodpecker (Picus miniaceus, Piciformes, Picidae), from Pennant, 1790 (40).

Japanese green woodpecker (Picus awokera, Piciformes, Picidae), from Temminck and Laugier de Chartrouse, 1820-39 (48).

Cuban green woodpecker (Xiphidiopicus percussus, Piciformes, Picidae), from Temminck and Laugier de Chartrouse, 1820-39 (48).

*Common flicker (*Colaptes auratus*) and red-headed woodpecker (*Melanerpes erythrocephalus, Piciformes, Picidae*), from Prévost and Lemaire, 1879 (43).*

*Top right, orange-backed woodpecker (*Reinwardtipicus validus, Piciformes, Picidae*), from Temminck and Laugier de Chartrouse, 1820-39 (48). Above, white-bellied black woodpecker (*Dryocopus javensis, Piciformes, Picidae*), from Temminck and Laugier de Chartrouse, 1820-39 (48).*

Below, helmeted woodpecker (Dryocopus galeatus, Piciformes, Picidae). Center, West Indian red-bellied woodpecker (Melanerpes superciliaris, Piciformes, Picidae). Top, orange-backed woodpecker (Reinwardtipicus validus, Piciformes, Picidae), all from Temminck and Laugier de Chartrouse, 1820-39 (48).

Victorian gentlemen, dignified ladies, and the editorial fate of exotic birds

The Victorian age saw in the field of naturalistic publications the flourishing of some large, important monographs dedicated to groups of brightly colored animals (usually birds and insects), with short but captivating scientific texts, and large ornamented plates with very accurate details of subjects and backgrounds.

The Englishman John Gould (1804-1881) is one of the most famous ornithologists and illustrators of this period. His publications include some of the most beautiful English naturalistic books, with drawings that were often addressed to an educated public of decidedly late-romantic taste. Gould started his carrer as a naturalist at Windsor, where his father was a gardener in the royal castle. In addition to botany, the young man devoted himself to zoology and taxidermy: this proved to be very useful to him later when he was employed by the English Zoological Society as chief taxidermist. Chronicles indicate that Gould had the honor to prepare and stuff the first giraffe ever brought to London; the poor animal had been sent as a present to King George IV and had died in the London Zoo. It seems that Gould's passion for exotic animals and his inclination to drawing, and arts in general, moved him to collect, into large monographs illustrated by himself or by his efficient collaborators, the new bird species brought back to the Zoological Society by English naturalists and travelers.

In addition, Gould had a marvelous aptitude for creating compositions in his pictures of animals; he knew well how to interpret the tastes of his time, giving symmetry to the subjects to be portrayed in his plates, and purposely choosing the rarest or most colorful species. Moreover, the backgrounds were always closely related to the birds or the zoological groups in the foreground: they often represented fruit or young shoots that the zoological species in question really liked to eat. Sometimes the portrayed subjects were carrying in their bills insects or other prey actually living in the areas they were inhabiting; nests and nestlings were never represented at random, but were carefully copied from life.

Gould also had the good luck to avail himself of specialized artists of great talent, who perfected with much good taste his "first ideas." Foremost among them was Gould's wife, Elisabeth, who quicky learned the difficult technique of lithography and transferred onto the lithographic stone, at the same time perfecting them, many of the animal sketches that her husband continued to draw on the preparatory sheet. A recent biographer reports that the extraordinary success of Gould's publications did not come from his charcoal sketches, often very vivid but rough, but rather from his extraordinary "intuition" in the organization of his collaborators' work, from his great enthusiasm, and from his extraordinary capacity for concentration while creating a new work of art. All these qualities allowed him to produce some of the greatest books on ornithology of all times.

The desire to portray new bird species never before described by naturalists, such as the avifaunas of Australia, Tasmania, and New Zealand, led Gould to emigrate with his wife and collaborators to the English colonies of the new "New World" for a couple of years. After reaching Tasmania in 1838, Gould left his wife at Hobart and proceeded toward the interior of the region, looking for new species to study and new ornithological subjects to portray. Later on, with the help of Gould's brother-in-law Coxen, the Goulds moved to New South Wales and from there John went on excursions, first around Sidney and then in southern Australia. On returning to England in 1840, most of the material for the first issues of *Birds of Australia* was ready, and three months later the work began to be published regularly. Very diplomatically, Gould succeeded in obtaining the patronage of Queen Victoria and the Prince Consort, Albert, to whom he had dedicated some new species of birds of paradise discovered in Australia. Furthermore, a large part of the English aristocracy started to contribute to this work with continuous financial help, facilitating the publication of additional parts of *Birds of Australia* which were then still in the course of preparation. A short time after coming back from Australia, Elisabeth Gould died. The task of lithographer was then entrusted to young Henry Richter, who continued transferring successfully onto lithographic stone Gould's preparatory drawings. In *Birds of Australia* Gould inaugurated the in-folio format for the drawings, having always a male and a female specimen portrayed for each species in cases of clear sexual dimorphism. When the two sexes were identical, Gould resorted to the expedient of portraying the animal in different attitudes and perspectives so as to give a clear idea of all the feather details. The background landscape became more and more detailed: skies and vaguely blue clouds were replaced, as the work was evolving and improving, by a landscape more true to reality, with plants and insects essential to the diet of the portrayed bird. According to Gould, each aspect of his compositions was of vital importance for the totality of the final picture; he thought that each detail of the drawing had to offer the public some naturalistic information about the animal's habits and habitat, as did the notes he wrote in pure "Victorian" style at the side of each plate.

Subsequent monographs about American partridges, European birds, Asian birds, and New Guinea birds were compiled accurately using the rules established by Gould for his great Australian work. However, the work that most pleased his public from the aesthetic point of view (see for instance the beautiful plate with the Brazilian ruby hummingbird at page 143) was perhaps the *Monograph of the Trochilidae or Family of Humming-birds*, published over the course of many years, from 1849 to 1860.

In his introduction to this monumental work on hummingbirds, Gould explains that, since boyhood, he had always been fascinated by the beauty of the feathers, the smallness of forms, and the dreams of faraway countries when admiring a tiny stuffed hummingbird. He had made friends with an English ornithologist, George Loddiges, who at the time owned one of the largest collections of Trochilidae of Great Britain. "How still vivid in my memory," Gould says, "the first hummingbird that met my ecstatic glance! With what delight I examined its tiny body and shiny feathers! My first impression became gradually a strong desire to acquire a deeper knowledge about this graceful group of the Trochilidae, and my desire became stronger and stronger when I had the opportunity to visit the collection of the late Mr. Loddiges of Hackney. This gentleman and I were both imbued with the same spirit of interest and fascination for the hummingbird family."

A few years later, in the course of a journey to America, to his great surprise Gould saw for the first time a live hummingbird, and this he remembers enthusiastically: "Then the time came when I had the opportunity to observe hummingbirds in nature, among the big blossoming trees of the United States and Canada. A hummingbird was for some time my faithful traveling companion, both on the road and on the train, and finally I succeeded in bringing back to England a living pair of these birds. I managed to keep one of them in London, but it survived only two days." The collection of hummingbirds that Gould managed to assemble later was one of the most spectacular ornithological treasures ever possessed by a private collector. Gould managed often to buy very rare species that were still unknown to science from explorers of the New World.

Lyrebirds, larks, swallows, blackbirds, nightingales, bullfinches, sparrows, birds of paradise, and crows

The order of Passeriformes, described in this chapter, includes as
many as sixty families and nearly 60 percent of all the bird
species living today. If then we consider the number of
individuals and their presence in the various environments, the
importance of Passeriformes must be considered even greater.
Many species are widely spread and thrive not only in
environments modified by man for agricultural purposes, but
also in urban and suburban environments as well. The reason
for this success can be found first of all in their small
dimensions and, second, in the extraordinary vocal capabilities
of the syrinx, which enables Passeriformes to utter very
elaborate sounds, always very different from one species to the
other. The various species, thanks to their small dimensions,
manage to occupy and share very efficiently the many ecological
niches available in the various environments, and, within the
limits of each species, song is a simple, economic, and efficient
way for the subdivision of territories among the males and for
sexual choice on the part of the females.

Since all the birds in this chapter belong to the order of Passeriformes the order indication has been omitted from the captions.
Right, long-tailed broadbill (Psarisomus dalhousiae, Eurylaimidae) and top right, black and yellow broadbill (Eurylaimus ochromalus, Eurylaimidae), both from Temminck and Laugier de Chartrouse, 1820-39 (48).

Above left, curve-billed scythebill (Campylorhamphus procurvoides, Dendrocolaptidae), from Temminck and Laugier de Chartrouse, 1820-39 (48). Above right, banded broadbill (Eurylaimus javanicus, Eurylaimidae), from Cuvier, 1836-49 (9).

Top left, green broadbill
(Calyptomena viridis,
Eurylaimidae), from Cuvier, 1836-
49 (9). Above, black-banded
woodcreeper (Dendrocolaptes
picumnus, Dendrocolaptidae),
from Zoological Society of London,
1870 (51). Left, dusky broadbill
(Corydon sumatranus,
Eurylaimidae), from Temminck and
Laugier de Chartrouse, 1820-39
(48).

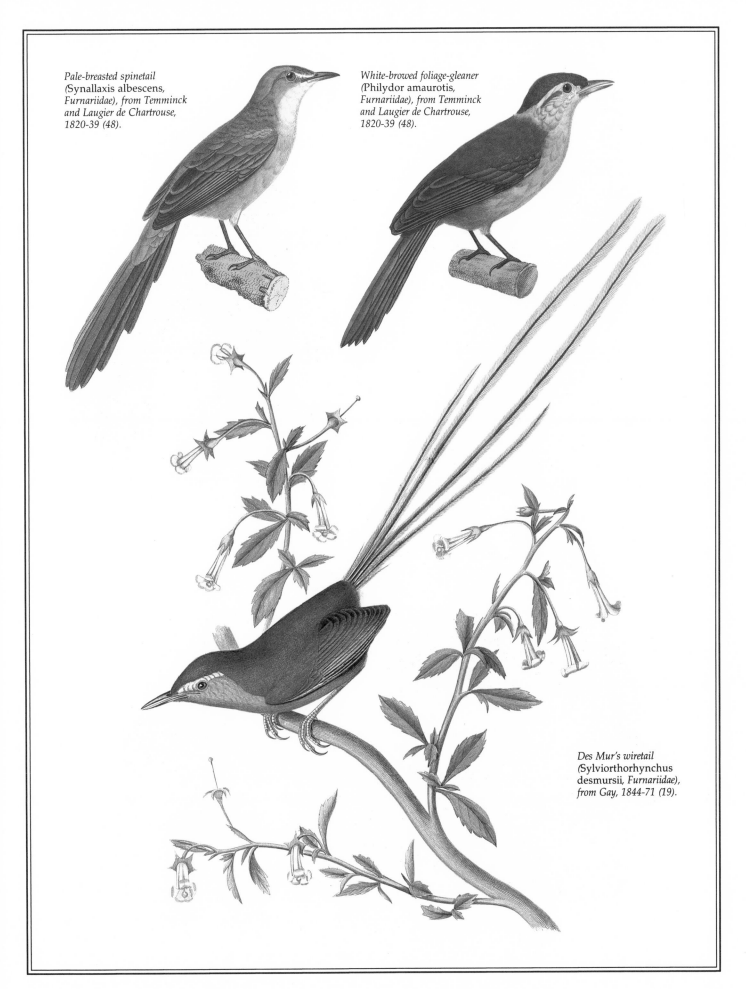

Pale-breasted spinetail (Synallaxis albescens, Furnariidae), from Temminck and Laugier de Chartrouse, 1820-39 (48).

White-browed foliage-gleaner (Philydor amaurotis, Furnariidae), from Temminck and Laugier de Chartrouse, 1820-39 (48).

Des Mur's wiretail (Sylviorthorhynchus desmursii, Furnariidae), from Gay, 1844-71 (19).

173

Above, lark-like brushrunner (Coryphistera alaudina, Furnariidae), from Zoological Society of London, 1870 (51). Below, yellow-browed antbird (Hypocnemis hypoxantha, Furnariidae), from Zoological Society of London, 1870 (51).

Recurvebill bushbird (Clytoctantes alixii, Furmicaridae), from Zoological Society of London, 1870 (51).

Gray-bellied spinetail (Synallaxis cinerascens, Furnariidae), from Temminck and Laugier de Chartrouse, 1820-39 (48).

Above left, slaty bristlefront (Merulaxis ater, Rhinocryptidae), from Lesson, 1830-32 (30). Top right, red-breasted pitta (Pitta erythrogaster, Pittidae), from Temminck and Laugier de Chartrouse, 1820-39 (48). Right, blue-tailed pitta (Pitta guajana, Pittidae), from Mueller, 1839-44 (38).

Above, blue-headed pitta (Pitta baudi, Pittidae), from Mueller, 1839-44 (38). Top right, garnet pitta (Pitta granatina, Pittidae), from Temminck and Laugier de Chartrouse, 1820-39 (48).

Left, giant pitta (Pitta caerulea) from Temminck and Laugier de Chartrouse, 1820-39 (48) and (below) Moluccan pitta (Pitta moluccensis, Pittidae), from Temminck and Laugier de Chartrouse, 1820-39 (48).

*Black Phoebe
(Sayornis nigricans,
Tyrannidae), from
Audubon, 1840-44 (2).*

*Above, streamer-tailed tyrant
(Gubernetes yetapa, Tyrannidae),
from Temminck and Laugier de
Chartrouse, 1820-39 (48). Left,
Amazonian royal flycatcher
(Onychorhynchus coronatus,
Tyrannidae), from Buffon, 1853-57 (5).*

Above, black-capped manakin (Piprites pileatus, Pipridae), from Donovan, 1834 (14). Center, streamer-tailed tyrant (Gubernates yetapa, Tyrannidae), from Temminck and Laugier de Chartrouse, 1820-39 (48). Top, red-headed manakin (Pipra rubrocapilla, Pipridae), from Temminck and Laugier de Chartrouse, 1820-39 (48).

Above right, bearded bellbird (Procnias averano, Cotingidae), from Temminck and Laugier de Chartrouse, 1820-39 (48). Top right, white bellbird (Procnias alba, Cotingidae), from Cuvier, 1836-49 (9). Below, barethroated bellbird (Procnias nudicollis, Cotingidae), from Temminck and Laugier de Chartrouse, 1820-39 (48).

*Right, Amazonian umbrellabird
(Cephalopterus ornatus,
Cotingidae), from Temminck and
Laugier de Chartrouse, 1820-39
(48). Center, swallow-tailed cotinga
(Phibalura flavirostris,
Cotingidae), from Temminck and
Laugier de Chartrouse, 1820-39
(48). Top right, Guianan cock of the
rock (Rupicola rupicola,
Cotingidae), from D'Orbigny, 1837
(15).*

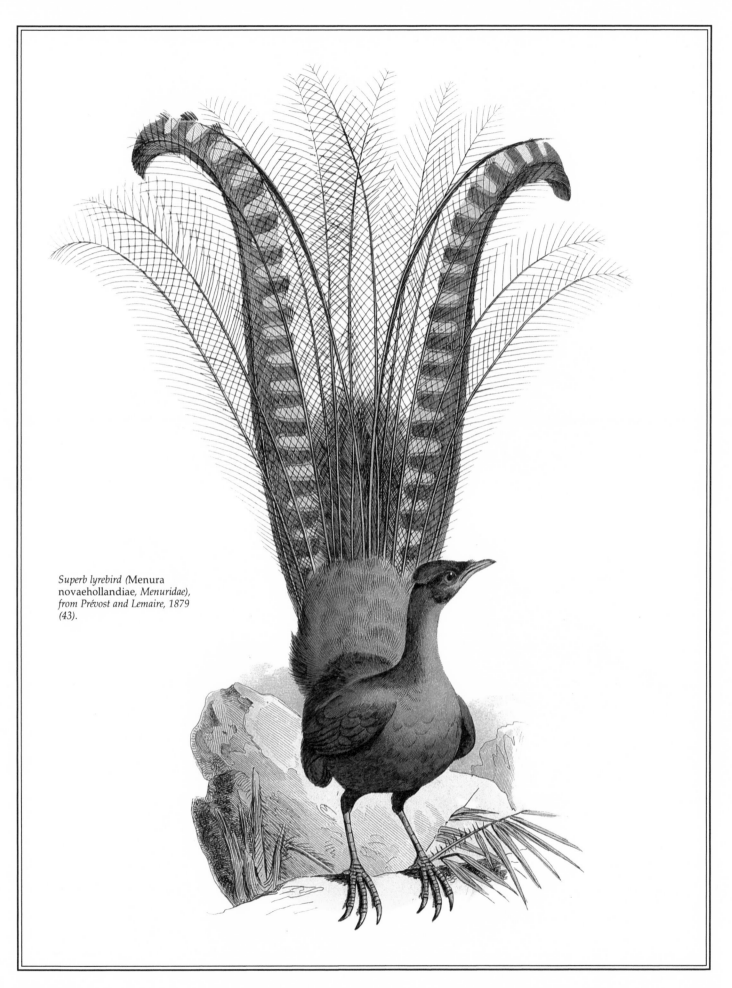

*Superb lyrebird (*Menura novaehollandiae, Menuridae*), from Prévost and Lemaire, 1879 (43).*

Singing bush lark (Mirafra javanica, Alaudidae), from Mathews, 1910-28 (35).

Above left, crested lark (Galerida cristata, Alaudidae), from Cuvier, 1836-49 (9). Above right, fawn-colored bush lark (Mirafra africanoides, Alaudidae), from Smith, 1838-49 (45). Right, Temminck's horned lark (Eremophila bilopha, Alaudidae), from Temminck and Laugier de Chartrouse, 1820-39 (48).

*Right, barn swallow (*Hirundo rustica, Hirundinidae*), from Buffon, 1853-57 (5). Below, yellow wagtail (*Motacilla flava, Motacillidae*), from Mathews, 1910-28 (35).*

Fournier sc.

*Below left, African river martin (*Pseudochelidon eurystomina, *Hirundinidae), from Dubois, 1905 (16). Below right, tawny-headed swallow (*Alopochelidon fucata, *Hirundinidae), from Temminck and Laugier de Chartrouse, 1820-39 (48).*

*Above, Angola swallow (*Hirundo angolensis, *Hirundinidae), from Zoological Society of London, 1870 (51). Right, barn swallow (*Hirundo rustica savignii, *Hirundinidae), from Dubois, 1905 (16).*

Above left, chestnut-eared bulbul (Hipsipetes amaurotis, Pycnonotidae), from Temminck and Laugier de Chartrouse, 1820-39 (48). Above right and right, short-billed minivets (Pericrocotus brevirostris, Campephagidae), from David, 1877 (10). Below, bearded greenbul (Criniger barbatus, Pycnonotidae), from Temminck and Laugier de Chartrouse, 1820-39 (48).

Left, Anderson's bulbul (Pycnonotus xanthorrhous, Pycnonotidae), from David, 1877 (10). Below, Jerdon's minivest (Pericrocotus erythropygius, Campephagidae), from Temminck and Laugier de Chartrouse, 1820-39 (48).

Wattled cuckoo shrike (Campephaga lobata, Campephagidae), from Temminck and Laugier de Chartrouse, 1820-39 (48).

Right, blue-backed fairy bluebird (Irena puella, Irenidae) and (below) female example, from Temminck and Laugier de Chartrouse, 1820-39 (48). Top right, golden-fronted leafbird (Chloropsis aurifrons, Irenidae), from Temminck and Laugier de Chartrouse, 1820-39 (48).

Woodchat shrike (Lanius senator, Laniidae), from Donovan, 1794-1819 (13).

Lesser green leafbird (Chloropsis cyanopogon, Irenidae), from Temminck and Laugier de Chartrouse, 1820-39 (48).

*Rosy-patched shrike (*Tchagra cruenta, Laniidae*), from Lesson, 1830-32 (30).*

*Great gray shrike (*Lanius excubitor, Laniidae*), from Donovan, 1794-1819 (13).*

*Above, Chinese great gray shrike (*Lanius sphenocercus, Laniidae*), from David, 1877 (10). Below, Bornean bristlehead (*Pityriasis gymnocephala, Laniidae*), from Cuvier, 1836-49 (9).*

*Helmet bird (*Eurycerus prevostii, *Vangidae), from Lesson, 1830-32 (30).*

*Above left, Bohemian waxwing (*Bombycilla garrulus, *Bombicillidae), from D'Orbigny, 1837 (15). Top right, Japanese waxwing (*Bombycilla japonica, *Bombicillidae), from David, 1877 (10).*

Right, Carolina wren (Thryothorus ludovicianus, Troglodytidae), from Vieillot, 1807 (49). Below left, wren (Troglodytes troglodytes, Troglodytidae), from Gould, 1850-83 (23). Below right, banded wren (Trythorus pleurostictus, Troglodytidae), from Zoological Society of London, 1870 (51).

Brown thrasher (Toxostoma rufum, Mimidae), from De Kay, 1844 (11).

Left, mountain accentor (Prunella montanella, Prunellidae), from David, 1877 (10). Above, maroon-backed accentor (Prunella immaculata, Prunellidae), from David, 1877 (10).

Northern mockingbird (Mimus polyglottus, Mimidae), from De Kay, 1844 (11).

*Japanese grey thrush (*Turdus cardis, *Turdidae), from Temminck and Laugier de Chartrouse, 1820-39 (48).*

Above left, maroon-backed accentor (Prunella immaculata, *Prunellidae), from Gould, 1850-83 (23). Right, Hodgson's grandala* (Grandala coelicolor, *Turdidae), from David, 1877 (10).*

*Dusky thrush (*Turdus naumanni, *Turdidae), from Temminck and Laugier de Chartrouse, 1820-39 (48).*

*Eastern bluebird (*Sialia sialis, *Turdidae), from De Kay, 1844 (11).*

*Above left, redstart (*Phoenicurus phoenicurus, *Turdidae), from Donovan, 1794-1819 (13). Above right, stonechat (*Saxicola torquata, *Turdidae), from Donovan, 1794-1819 (13).*

*Blackbird (*Turdus merula, *Turdidae), from Cuvier, 1836-49 (9).*

*Left, Sunda whistling thrush (*Myiophoneus glaucinus, *Turdidae), from Temminck and Laugier de Chartrouse, 1820-39 (48).*

*Above, Kuhl's ground thrush (*Zoothera interpres, *Turdidae), from Temminck and Laugier de Chartrouse, 1820-39 (48). Below right, redbellied thrush (*Turdus chrysolaus, *Turdidae), from Temminck and Laugier de Chartrouse, 1820-39 (48).*

*Blue rock thrush (*Monticola solitarius, *Turdidae), from David, 1877 (10).*

*Above, thrush nightingale (*Luscinia luscinia, *Turdidae), from Donovan, 1794-1819 (13). Top right, nightingale (*Luscinia megarhynchos, *Turdidae), from Donovan, 1794-1819 (13). Below, European robin (*Erithacus rubecula, *Turdidae), from Donovan, 1794-1819 (13).*

Above left, Japanese robin (Erithacus akahige, Turdidae), from Temminck and Laugier de Chartrouse, 1820-39 (48). Right, Siberian blue robin (Erithacus cyane, Turdidae), from David, 1877 (10).

Riukiu robin (Erithacus komadori, Turdidae), from Temminck and Laugier de Chartrouse, 1820-39 (48).

Spotted forktail (Enicurus maculatus, Turdidae), from Gould, 1850-83 (23).

Right, streak-throated fulvetta (Alcippe cinereiceps, Timalidae), from David, 1877 (10).

Left, Ajax quail thrush (Cinclosoma ajax, Orthonychidae), from Temminck and Laugier de Chartrouse, 1820-39 (48).

Above, Malay rail babbler (Eupetes macrocerus, Orthonychidae), from Temminck and Laugier de Chartrouse, 1820-39 (48). Below, lowland rail babbler (Ptilorrhoa caerulescens, Orthonychidae), from Temminck and Laugier de Chartrouse, 1820-39 (48).

Left, crimson-winged laughing thrush (Garrulax formosus, Timalidae), from David, 1877 (10).

Peking robin (Leiothrix lutea, Timalidae), from David, 1877 (10).

Melodious laughing thrush (Garrulax canorus, Timalidae), from David, 1877 (10).

Top, great reed warbler (Acrocephalus arundinaceus, Sylviidae), from Morris, 1851-57 (37). Right, lesser whitethroat (Sylvia curruca, Sylviidae), from Donovan, 1794-1819 (13). Far right, blue wren warbler (Todopsis cyanocephala, Maluridae), from Gould, 1857-88 (24).

*White-faced chat
(Ephthianura
tricolor, Maluridae),
from Gould, 1840-48
(21).*

*Long-tailed tailor bird
(Orthotomus sutorius,
Sylviidae), from Pennant,
1790 (40).*

*Golden-crowned kinglet
(Regulus satrapa,
Sylviidae), from De Kay,
1844 (11).*

*Below left, Narcissus flycatcher (*Ficedula narcissina, *Muscicapidae*), *from Temminck and Laugier de Chartrouse, 1820-39 (48).*

Above and right, crested shrike tit (Falcunculus frontatus, *Muscicapidae*), *from Temminck and Laugier de Chartrouse, 1820-39 (48). Below left, blue and white flycatcher (*Cyanoptila cyanomelana, *Muscicapidae*), *from David, 1877 (10). Below right, rufous fantail (*Rhipidura rufifrons, *Muscicapidae*), *from Gould, 1875-88 (24).*

Left, African paradise flycatcher (Terpsiphone viridis, Muscicapidae), from Dubois, 1905 (16). Below, Mugimaki flycatcher (Ficedula mugimaki, Muscicapidae), from Temminck and Laugier de Chartrouse, 1820-39 (48).

Above left, black paradise flycatcher (Terpsiphone atrocaudata, Muscicapidae), from Temminck and Laugier de Chartrouse, 1820-39 (48). Right, Asiatic paradise flycatcher (Terpsiphone paradisi, Muscicapidae), from David, 1877 (10).

Below left, great tit (Parus ater, Paridae), from Donovan, 1794-1819 (13). Below right, blue tit (Parus caeruleus, Paridae), from Buffon, 1853-57 (5).

Left, European nuthatch (Sitta europaea, Sittidae), from Donovan, 1794-1819 (13). Above, Chinese yellow tit (Parus spilonotus, Paridae), from David, 1877 (10).

White-throated treecreeper (Climacteris leucophaea, Climacteridae), from Temminck and Laugier de Chartrouse, 1820-39 (48).

Brown treecreeper (Climacteris picumnus, Climacteridae), from Temminck and Laugier de Chartrouse, 1820-39 (48).

Above left, Himalayan treecreeper (Certhia himalayana, Certhiidae), from David, 1877 (10). Right, wallcreeper (Tichodroma muraria, Tichodromadidae), from Cuvier, 1836-49 (9).

*Yellow-throated flowerpecker (*Prionochilus maculatus, *Dicaeidae), from Temminck and Laugier de Chartrouse, 1820-39 (48).*

*Crimson-breasted flowerpecker (*Prionochilus percussus, *Dicaeidae), from Temminck and Laugier de Chartrouse, 1820-39 (48).*

*Left, scarlet-backed flowerpecker (*Dicaeum cruentatum, *Dicaeidae), from Gould, 1850-83 (23).*

*Above left and right, spotted pardalote (*Pardalotus punctatus, *Dicaeidae), from Temminck and Laugier de Chartrouse, 1820-39 (48).*

Below left, Mrs. Gould's sunbird (Aethopyga gouldiae, Nectariniidae), from David, 1877 (10). Below right, mouse-colored sunbird (Nectarinia veroxii, Nectariniidae), from Smith, 1838-49 (45).

Scarlet sunbird (Aethopyga mysticalis, Nectariniidae), from Temminck and Laugier de Chartrouse, 1820-39 (48).

Splendid sunbird (Nectarinia coccinigastra, Nectariniidae), from Temminck and Laugier de Chartrouse, 1820-39 (48).

Lesser yellow-eared spiderhunter (Arachnotera chrysogenys, Nectariniidae), from Temminck and Laugier de Chartrouse, 1820-39 (48).

*Tui (*Prosthemadura novaeseelandiae, *Meliphagidae), from Cuvier, 1836-49 (9).*

*Kauai O-o (*Moho braccatus, *Meliphagidae), from Temminck and Laugier de Chartrouse, 1820-39 (48).*

*Above left, chestnut-flanked white eye (*Zosterops erytropleura, *Zosteropidae), from David, 1877 (10). Right, yellow wattle bird (*Anthochaera paradoxa, *Meliphagidae), from Mathews, 1910-28 (35).*

*Below left, reed bunting (*Emberiza schoeniclus, *Emberizidae). Below right, ortolan bunting (*Emberiza hortulana, *Emberizidae), both from Buffon, 1853-57 (5).*

*Above left, pine bunting (*Emberiza leucocephala, *Emberizidae), from Donovan, 1794-1819 (13). Above right, common cardinal (*Cardinalis cardinalis, *Emberizidae), from Prévost and Lemaire, 1879 (43).*

*Top left, seven-colored tanager (*Tangara fastuosa, Emberizidae*), from Lesson, 1830-32 (30). Top right, blue-grey tanager (*Thraupis episcopus, Emberizidae*), from Prévost and Lemaire, 1879 (43). Above, emerald tanager (*Tangara florida, Emberizidae*), from Zoological Society of London, 1870 (51).*

*Diademed tanager (*Stephanophorus diadematus, Emberizidae*), from Temminck and Laugier de Chartrouse, 1820-39 (48).*

*Top, grey-chested greenlet (*Hylophilus semicinereus, *Vireonidae), from Zoological Society of London, 1870 (51). Center, Montezuma oropendola (*Psarocolius montezuma, *Vireonidae), from Lesson, 1830-32 (30). Right, brambling (*Fringilla montifringilla, *Fringillidae), from Donovan, 1794-1819 (13).*

Lichtenstein's oriole (Icterus
gularis, Icteridae), from Lesson,
1830-32 (30).

Red-breasted blackbird
(Sturnella militaris, Icteridae),
from Gay, 1844-71 (19).

Canary (Serinus canaria,
Fringillidae), from Buffon, 1853-57
(5).

Below left, European goldfinch (Carduelis carduelis, Fringillidae), from Donovan, 1794-1819 (13). Below, masked hawfinch (Coccothraustes personatus, Fringillidae), from David, 1877 (10).

Above left, three-banded rosefinch (Carpodacus trifasciatus, Fringillidae), from David, 1877 (10). Above, Oriental greenfinch (Carduelis sinica, Fringillidae), from Temminck and Laugier de Chartrouse, 1820-39 (48).

*Below left, European hawfinch (*Coccothraustes coccothraustes*) and (below right) red crossbill (*Loxia curvirostra, Fringillidae), *from Buffon, 1853-57 (5).*

*Above left, red crossbill (*Loxia curvirostra, Fringillidae*), from Cuvier, 1836-49 (9). Right, bullfinch (*Pyrrhula pyrrhula, Fringillidae*), from Donovan, 1794-1819 (13).*

Gouldian finch (Chloebia gouldiae, Estrildidae), from Mathews, 1910-28 (35).

Below left, red-cheeked cordon bleu (Uraeginthus bengalus, Estrildidae), from Donovan, 1834 (14). Below right, long-tailed whydah (Euplectes progne, Ploceidae), from Prévost and Lemaire, 1879 (43).

Left, golden-backed weaver (Ploceus jacksoni, Ploceidae), from Comte, 1830 (7). Above, sociable weaver (Philetairus socius, Ploceidae), from Smith, 1838-49 (45).

Scaly weaver (Sporopipes squamifrons, Ploceidae), from Smith, 1838-49 (45).

Shining starling (Aplonis metallica, Sturnidae), from Temminck and Laugier de Chartrouse, 1820-39 (48).

Above, tree sparrow (Passer montanus, Ploceidae), from Donovan, 1794-1819 (13). Right, paradise sparrow (Amadina erythrocephala, Ploceidae), from Smith, 1838-49 (45).

*Silky starling (*Sturnus sericeus, *Sturnidae), from David, 1877 (10).*

*Grey starling (*Sturnus cineraceus, *Sturnidae), from Temminck and Laugier de Chartrouse, 1820-39 (48).*

*Above, Celebes enodes starling (*Enodes erythrophris, *Sturnidae), from Temminck and Laugier de Chartrouse, 1820-39 (48). Below, red-billed oxpecker (*Buphagus erythrorhynchus, *Sturnidae), from Temminck and Laugier de Chartrouse, 1820-39 (48).*

*Great sparrow (*Passer motitensis, *Ploceidae), from Smith, 1838-49 (45).*

Above left, uja (Heteralocha acutirostris, Callaeidae), from Gould, 1840-48 (21). Above right, greater racquet-tailed drongo (Dicrurus paradiseus, Dicruridae), from Cuvier, 1836-49 (9). Below, golden oriole (Oriolus oriolus, Oriolidae), from Cuvier, 1836-49 (9).

Crested mynah (Acridotheres cristatellus, Sturnidae), from David, 1877 (10).

Bismarck wood swallow (Artamus insignis, Artamidae), from Gould, 1875-88 (24).

White-winged chough (Corcorax melanorhamphos, Grallinidae), from Mathews, 1910-28 (35).

Below, black butcher bird (Cracticus quoyi, Cracticidae), from Gould, 1875-88 (24).

Above left, green catbird (Ailuroedus crassirostris, Ptilonorhynchidae), from Mathews, 1910-28 (35).

Below left, Newton's golden bowerbird (Prionodura newtoniana, Ptilonorhynchidae), from Mathews, 1910-28 (35). Below, spotted bowerbird (Chlamydera maculata, Ptilonorhynchidae), from Mathews, 1910-28 (35).

Below, satin bowerbird (Ptilonorhynchus violaceus, Ptilonorhynchidae), from Mathews, 1910-28 (35).

*Right, flamed bowerbird (*Sericulus aureus, *Ptilonorhynchidae), from Lesson, 1853 (31). Below right, magnificent riflebird (*Ptiloris magnificus, *Paradisaeidae), from Mathews, 1910-28 (35).*

*Above, trumpet bird (*Phonygammus keraudrenii, *Paradisaeidae), from Mathews, 1910-28 (35).*

*Regent bowerbird (*Sericulus chrysocephalus, *Ptilonorhynchidae), from Lesson, 1853 (31).*

Red bird of paradise (Paradisea rubra, Paradisaeidae),
from Levaillant, 1806 (33) and from Lesson, 1853 (31).

Greater bird of paradise (Paradisaea apoda, Paradisaeidae), from Levaillant, 1806 (33), and from Lesson, 1853 (31).

Lesser bird of paradise (Paradisaea minor, Paradisaeidae), from Lesson, 1853 (31), and from Gray, 1830-34 (25).

Top left, Arfak parotia (Parotia sefilata, Paradisaeidae), from Lesson, 1853 (31). Above, Arfak bird of paradise (Astrapia nigra, Paradisaeidae), from Lesson, 1853 (31).

Superb bird of paradise (Lophorina superba, Paradisaeidae), from Lesson, 1853 (31).

Above, black sicklebill (Epimachus fastosus, Paradisaeidae), from Lesson, 1853 (31). Below, magnificent bird of paradise (Diphyllodes magnificus, Paradisaeidae), from Dubois, 1905 (16).

Above, blue jay (Cyanocitta cristata, Corvidae), from Levaillant, 1806 (33). Right, white-throated magpie-jay (Calocitta formosa, Corvidae), from Temminck and Laugier de Chartrouse, 1820-39 (48).

Left, azure-winged magpie (Cyanopica cyana, Corvidae), from David, 1877 (10). Right, red-billed blue magpie (Urocissa erythrorhyncha, Corvidae), from David, 1877 (10).

*Southern tree pie (*Dendrocitta leucogastra, *Corvidae),
from Zoological Society of London, 1870 (51).*

*Above, magpie (*Pica pica,
*Corvidae), from Donovan, 1794-
1819 (13).*

*Left, Cuban crow (*Corvus nasicus, *Corvidae). Above, bushy crested jay
(*Cissilopha melanocyanea, *Corvidae), both from Temminck and Laugier de
Chartrouse, 1820-39 (48).*

Amid the shadows of the forest, the search for the bird of paradise

Among all Passeriformes, no doubt the birds of paradise of the Australian-Papua area have especially attracted the attention of naturalists and artists thanks to their incredible feathers and their gorgeous colors. Several monographs have been published with plenty of color plates from the early 19th century to today, and in New Guinea naturalists have always tried to learn more about the biology of these marvelous birds by observing them "from life." The fact that 16th-century seafarers bought skins of birds of paradise without legs (and sometimes even without wings) led to the legend that these birds had no legs and never rested on the ground, but went on flying uninterruptedly, even in sleep. Moreover, it was a common belief that they used to cling for a short while to tree branches with the long tendrils of their tails and coupled in flight. It was also believed that the laying and hatching of eggs would take place in flight, that the male had a hollow on his back into which the female laid her eggs, and that the same female would hatch them with the help of a corresponding hollow in her abdomen. In order to make this "position" steady, male and female would interlace their tail tendrils — still in flight. In addition, the birds of paradise were believed (and this too was put in writing) never to feed, but to live off of steam and dew and to have the abdominal cavity full only of fat, with no stomach or intestine. In effect, such organs would be completely useless to birds that never ate anything and would never have to digest or evacuate. In short, the birds of paradise lived flying continuously in the sky, almost "swimming" in the air, with the help of their axillary feathers, and never touched ground except at death. In the late 17th century and in the 18th century a few of these birds were brought to Europe complete with legs, discrediting the legend. The great Linnaeus called *apodal* ("without feet") one of the finest species of these birds as a remem-

brance of the extravagant descriptions of the ancient seafarers, but the life habits of these passeriformes still remained totally unknown to competent European science. Thanks to some stuffed specimens existing in the rich museums of France and Holland, the naturalist Levaillant published in 1806 some beautiful pictures of birds of paradise, based on original drawings by Barraband (see the red bird of paradise at page 223). But the text accompanying them said little or nothing about the life habits of the bird of paradise.

Only twenty years later, with the increase of discoveries and exploration voyages in the South Seas, were naturalists able to observe and capture a few birds of paradise in their natural habitat. The French corvette *Coquille*, captained by Duperrey, had two naturalists on board when it sailed from the port of Toulon on August 11, 1821: they were the medical officer P. Garnot and the naval chemist René-Primevère Lesson. Both were appointed by the Paris museum to effect collections of natural history materials during the voyage, of course tending at the same time to their own medical appointments. After rounding Cape Horn, the *Coquille* proceeded into the Pacific Ocean, visiting the Moluccas and stopping at Port Jackson in Australia for repairs in 1824. Here Garnot was compelled by an illness to return to Europe in haste. Taking advantage of the departure of a merchant ship, all the scientific materials collected until that moment were entrusted to him, whereas the *Coquille* would resume her exploration voyages. But Garnot was not lucky: in July 1824 the merchant ship was shipwrecked, the collections were swallowed up by the waves, and he barely succeeded in saving his life.

Meanwhile, the *Coquille* reached New Zealand, touched the Caroline Islands, and stopped in the Papua port of Dorey, where Lesson carried out land excursions from July 20 to August 9, 1824, collecting animals and making naturalistic observations. He was fascinated by New Guinea and even more by the birds of paradise, which for the first time he was able to see in the wild. The natives brought him new species of birds that, once back home, he would describe. About the minor bird of paradise, Lesson wrote: "The minor bird of paradise has quick agile movements, and the same habits as the birds of the family of magpies. In the forests where it lives it searches out the tops of the tallest trees and comes down to the medium-height branches to look for food or for protection from the sun; it fears heat and loves the shade of the thick leaves of teak trees. It seldom leaves these trees in the middle of the day, and it can be seen going about in search of food only in the mornings and evenings. Usually, when it thinks it is alone, it utters a sharp cry, frequently repeated, which can be imitated with the syllables *voake voake voako*, uttered in a loud voice. This cry, at the time of our stay in New Guinea, i.e., in July, appeared to be meant to call females, assembled together in groups of about twenty individuals, calling back from the surrounding trees and answering this love call. We never saw more than one male in these groups of females, all plain and with no ornaments, whereas he, a dandy with feathers, looked like a cock crowing over an opponent after winning supremacy over the henhouse. Attracted and guided by their cries *voake voako* we could easily follow and kill many of them in the course of our hunts. The first specimen we saw left us so astonished that we didn't even think of using our guns, so great was our amazement. We were proceeding cautiously along the paths frequented by wild pigs, deep inside the thick shady forests near Dorey, when a male of this species passed over our heads, flying with grace and ease, with sudden slight jerks; it looked like a meteor that with its flaming tail leaves a long streak of light behind itself. This bird of paradise, which carried its long side feathers pressed against its sides, resembled a plume that had got loose from the hair of a *houri* and balanced softly on the air layer that envelopes the earth crust of our planet."

Even hunting birds of paradise roused Lesson's curiosity and enabled him to study the hunting techniques of the natives, who used (and still do) bird of paradise's plumes for their ritual ornaments. "When an unusual noise reaches the ears of the minor bird of paradise, its cries cease, its movements stop, and it stands absolutely still, hidden in the thick of the leaves that protect it from the hunters' sight; but if the noise continues, it doesn't hesitate to fly away. It perches onto the highest branches of the tallest trees, and it is very difficult to hit it, unless one is equipped with a long-range gun, as it does not fall to the ground unless it is shot dead, and it is impossible to shoot at it from a distance of less than a hundred fifty steps. If it is only wounded, the bird of paradise hides to die inside thick shrubs; however, one day we found by the border of a water pool, in the bed of a half-dried stream, one of these birds that had been wounded the day before. It is in the evenings, or better, in the mornings, that the hunter must lie in wait, after choosing carefully trees full of fruit, on the branches of which the birds alight. There he must wait patiently, absolutely motionless, for the arrival of the birds of paradise, which with their sharp sudden cries will reveal at once their presence."

Lesson's work describing these superb birds was published in 1835, with 43 plates by the painters Pretre and Oudart, hand engraved and colored, with the title *Histoire Naturelle des oiseaux de paradis et des épimaques* (see for example the black sicklebill at page 226), and it constitutes one of the richest examples of the French naturalistic publications of the time.

The Sources

The color prints of birds in this book are taken from the following famous ornithological works. The numbers used in the captions correspond to the numbers above each title.

1. Albin, Cleazar
A natural history of birds. Illustrated with copper plates, curiously engraven from the life. And exactly colour'd by the author. To which are added notes and observations by W. Derham. London, 1731-38. P. 106

2. Audubon, John James Laforest
The birds of America; from drawings made in the United States and their territories. New York and Philadelphia, 1840-44. P. 177

3. Bree, Charles Robert
A history of the birds of Europe, not observed in the British Isles. London, 1859-63. P. 32

4. Buffon, George-L.L., Comte de
Historie naturelle générale et particulière. Nouvelle édition accompagnée de notes, rédigée par C.S. Sonnini. Paris, 1799-1808. P. 25

5. Buffon, George-L.L., Comte de
Oeuvres complètes avec la nomenclature linnéenne et la classification de Cuvier; revisées sur l'édition in 4° de l'Imprimerie Royale et annotées par M. J.P. Flourens. Paris, 1853-57. Pp. 26, 32, 34, 41, 43, 60, 62, 81, 87, 88, 96, 97, 106, 108, 109, 120, 122, 146, 159, 160, 177, 183, 204, 209, 212, 214

6. Catesby, Mark
The natural history of Carolina, Florida and the Bahama Islands, containing the figures of birds, beasts, fishes, serpentes, insects and plants; particularly the forest-trees, shrubs, and other plants, not hitherto described or very incorrectly figured by authors. London, 1754. Pp. 33, 46, 104

7. Comte, Joseph-Achille
Musée d'histoire naturelle comprenant la cosmographie, la géologie, la zoologie, la botanique. Paris, 1830. Pp. 140, 203, 216

8. Cory, Charles Barney
The birds of Haiti and San Domingo. Boston, 1885. Pp. 103, 148

9. Cuvier, Georges-Léopold-Chrétien-Frédéric-Dagobert
Le Règne Animal distribué d'après son organisation. Paris, 1836-49. Pp. 21, 25, 26, 28, 29, 31, 36, 37, 38, 41, 43, 44, 46, 55, 57, 69, 71, 90, 92, 96, 104, 105, 106, 107, 110, 111, 112, 115, 121, 147, 153, 154, 171, 172, 182, 188, 194, 195, 205, 208, 214, 219

10. David, abbé Armand et Oustalet, Emile
Les oiseaux de la Chine. Paris, 1877. Pp. 39, 76, 80, 82, 83, 85, 87, 110, 122, 138, 185, 186, 188, 189, 191, 192, 194, 196, 198, 201, 202, 204, 205, 207, 208, 213, 218, 219, 227

11. De Kay, J.E.
Zoology of New York, part II. Birds. New York, 1844. Pp. 30, 191, 193, 200

12. Des Murs, Marc-Athanase-Parfait-Oeillet
Iconographie ornithologique. Nouveau recueil général des planches peintes d'oiseaux, pour servir de suite et de complément aux planches enluminées de Buffon et aux planches coloriées de Temminck et Laugier de Chartouse. Figures dessinées et peintes par Alphonse Prévost et Oudart. Paris, 1845-49. Pp. 71, 78

13. Donovan, Edward
The natural history of British birds or a selection of the most rare, beautiful and interesting birds. London, 1794-1819. Pp. 26, 35, 40, 44, 45, 66, 68, 69, 93, 94, 95, 107, 108, 114, 136, 137, 151, 163, 187, 188, 193, 195, 199, 204, 209, 211, 213, 214, 217, 228

14. Donovan, Edward
The naturalist's repository or miscellany of exotic natural history, exhibiting rare and beautiful specimens of foreign birds, insects, shells, quadrupeds, fishes and marine productions, more especially such new subjects as have not hitherto been figured or correctly described. London, 1834. Pp. 125, 126, 145, 157, 162, 178, 216

15. D'Orbigny, Alcide Dessalines
Dictionaire universel d'Histoire naturelle. Paris, 1837. Pp. 25, 35, 42, 45, 52, 57, 86, 114, 147, 155, 161, 180, 189

16. Dubois, Alphonse-Joseph-Charles
Remarques sur l'ornithologie de l'État indépendant du Congo suivies d'une liste des espèces recueillies jusqu'ici dans cet état. Brussels, 1905. Pp. 141, 158, 184, 202, 226

17. Edwards, George
A natural history of birds. London, 1743-51. P. 135

18. Gaimard, Joseph-Paul
Voyage en Islande et au Groënland exécuté pendant les années 1835 et 1836 sur la corvette La Recherche comandée par M. Tréhouart, pubblié par orde du Roi. Paris, 1838-52. Pp. 69, 107, 113, 116

19. Gay, Claude
Historia fisica y politica de Chile. Santiago and Paris, 1844-71. Pp. 4, 43, 64, 66, 96, 173, 212

20. Gould, John
A monograph of the Trogonidae or family of trogons. London, 1838. P. 148

21. Gould, John
The birds of Australia. London, 1840-48. Pp. 22, 90, 200, 219.

22. Gould, John
A monograph of the Trochilidae or family of hummingbirds. London, 1849-61. Pp. 143, 144

23. Gould, John
The birds of Asia. Completed after the author's death by R. Bowdler Sharpe. London, 1850-83. Pp. 103, 112, 114, 154, 190, 192, 197, 206

24. Gould, John
The birds of New Guinea and the adjacent Papuan Islands, including many new species recently discovered in Australia. London, 1875-88. Pp. 140, 141, 199, 201, 220

25. Gray, John Edward
Illustrations of Indian zoology chiefly selected from the collection of Maj.-Gen. Hardwicke. London, 1830-34. Pp. 53, 54, 58, 88, 139, 142, 224

26. Grønvold, Henrik and Swann, Harry Kirke
Illustrations of the game birds and water fowl of South America. London, 1915-17. Pp. 21, 23, 24, 26, 70, 72, 95

27. Leach, William Elford
The zoological miscellany, being descriptions of new or interesting animals. London, 1814-17. Pp. 31, 34, 133

28. Lesson, René-Primevère
Voyage autour du monde sur la Coquille pendant 1822-25. Paris, 1826-30. P. 134

29. Lesson, René-Primevère
Histoire naturelle des oiseaux-mouches, ouvrage orné de planches dessinées et gravées par les meilleurs artistes. Paris, 1829-30. Pp. 145, 146, 147

30. Lesson, René-Primevère
Centurie Zoologique. Paris, 1830-32. Pp. 58, 72, 111, 152, 175, 188, 189, 210, 211, 212

31. Lesson, René-Primevère
Histoire naturelle des oiseaux de paradis et des épimaques. Paris, 1835. Pp. 222, 223, 224, 225, 226

32. Levaillant, François
Histoire naturelle des perroquets. Paris, 1801-05. Pp. 125, 126

33. Levaillant, François
Histoire naturelle des oiseaux de paradis et des rolliers, suivie de celle des toucans et des barbus. Paris, 1806. Pp. 223, 227

34. Loche, Victor
Exploration scientifique de l'Algérie pendant 1840-42. Paris, 1844-67. P. 98

35. Mathews, Gregory Macalister
The birds of Australia. London, 1910-28. Pp. 182, 183, 208, 215, 220, 221, 222

36. Meyer, Henry Leonard
Coloured illustrations of British birds and their eggs. London, 1853-57. P. 67

37. Morris, Francis Orpen
A history of British birds. London, 1851-57. P. 199

38. Mueller, Salomon
Verhandelingen over de natuurlijke geschiedenis der Nederlandsche overzeesche bezittingen, door de leden der Natuurkundige Commissie in Indië en andere schrijvers. Leiden, 1839-44. Pp. 157, 175, 176

39. Mulsant, Martial-Etienne et Verreaux, Edouard
Histoire naturelle des oiseaux-moches ou colibris constituant la famille des Trochilidés. Lyons, 1874-77. P. 145

40. Pennant, Thomas
Indian zoology. London, 1790. Pp. 73, 137, 164, 200

41. Pennant, Thomas
Outlines of the Globe. London, 1798-1800. P. 75

42. Pouchet, F.-A.
Zoologie classique ou Histoire naturelle du règne animal. Paris, 1841. Pp. 38, 42, 68, 118

43. Prévost, Florent et Lemaire, C.L.
Histoire naturelle des oiseaux exotiques. Paris, 1879. Pp. 122, 131, 133, 134, 147, 154, 158, 159, 165, 181, 209, 210, 216

44. Selby, Prideaux John
Natural history of parrots. Edinburgh, 1836. P. 121

45. Smith, Andrew
Illustrations of the Zoology of South Africa. London, 1838-49. Pp. 30, 57, 131, 135, 136, 137, 138, 151, 153, 182, 207, 216, 217, 218

46. Susemihl, Johann Conrad
Abbildungen der Vögel Europas, herausgegeben, gezeichnet und in Stahl gestochen. Stuttgart, Darmstadt, and Leipzig, 1839-51. P. 57

47. Takagi, Shunzan
Honno Zusetsu. Edo, late Edo period (1603-1867). P. 41

48. Temminck, Coenraad Jacob et Laugier de Chartrouse, Meiffren
Nouveau recueil de planches coloriées d'oiseaux pour servir de suite et de complément aux planches enluminées de Buffon, d'après dessins de Huet et Prête. Paris, 1820-39. Pp. 23, 24, 27, 28, 29, 32, 34, 36, 38, 39, 40, 42, 45, 51, 52, 54, 55, 56, 58, 59, 60, 61, 62, 63, 64, 65, 68, 70, 72, 73, 74, 76, 77, 78, 79, 81, 83, 84, 89, 90, 91, 92, 93, 94, 97, 104, 105, 108, 110, 111, 112, 113, 116, 117, 118, 119, 120, 121, 123, 124, 131, 132, 133, 134, 135, 136, 137, 138, 139, 140, 142, 148, 149, 150, 151, 152, 154, 156, 157, 159, 160, 161, 162, 163, 164, 165, 166, 171, 172, 173, 174, 175, 176, 177, 178, 179, 180, 182, 184, 185, 186, 187, 192, 194, 196, 198, 201, 202, 205, 206, 207, 208, 210, 213, 217, 218, 227, 228

49. Viellot, L.-J.P.
Histoire Naturelle des Oiseaux de l'Amérique Septentrionale. Paris, 1807. Pp. 52, 56, 190

50. Wolf, Josef
Zoological Sketches. Edited by D.W. Mitchel and P.L. Sclater. London, 1861-67. P. 37

51. Zoological Society of London
Proceedings of the Scientific Meetings. London, 1861-90. Pp. 24, 25, 31, 74, 79, 80, 94, 98, 126, 141, 150, 158, 172, 174, 184, 190, 210, 211, 228

Latin Names of the Species

English Names of the Species